# WISH

# PROOF

## LALANII ROCHELLE

"Wildflowers" first appeared in *The Scrambler.*

"Beautiful Again," aka "Fucked" first appeared in *The Citron Review* in a different form.  Cover Image By Casey Sklar of Hand Me Down Art @_hand_me_down_.

FOR DADDY

I KNOW YOU'VE GONE FISHING AND
I'M TOO LATE,

BUT HERE'S SOMETHING FOR YOU TO
READ AT THE LAKE WHILE YOU'RE
WAITING FOR ME.

I LOVE YOU,

LALANII

# TABLE OF CONTENTS

VI

# CHAPTER 1

# PREGNORANT

I sat in the waiting room of the abortion clinic. Daddy sat next to me, cool as prescription glasses with a tint. No words. Lines in his beige forehead gleamed with perspiration. Flushes of fear radiated through my blood. I had crippling constipation and occasional piss parties (porcelain and I were good friends). I had to pee ten times in two hours. It was the middle of May, and I was fifteen. 1999. I had never ridden a train, gone to an aquarium, taken a trip without my mom and dad, been to an art museum, or gone to a movie by myself, and yet I was pregnant.

White walls held my attention, the way an ellipsis waits in the wrong place. I gripped the cold metal chair as if it would give me air. Forgiveness wasn't growling in my stomach, but maybe I'd call him collect again later. Nurse Whoever smiled pityingly.

A pale woman in a white coat and old carpet–brown hair called my last name. "Grant."

I looked up.

Few people in the waiting room glanced; everyone knew not to stare. This was a secret society of silence and compliance. I walked through the door slowly. I walked through the second door more slowly. Left my father in the waiting room, and my heart began to panic, adrenaline pumping like a kitchen fire as it spreads to the bedroom, and your entire life is in that bedroom, but in this case, my entire life was in my abdomen. Left my father in the waiting room the way he would soon leave me, begging for forgiveness. Left my father in the waiting room with the white, white walls the color of shock and the smell of needles and problems. Left my father in the waiting room, waiting for what I'd done to be undone. Left my father in the waiting room because after all, all of the fathers wait in the waiting room. Eyes wet, but I blinked, emotionless.

When I was a child, I would always pretend I had wings. Except they weren't really wings—they were only pillowcases tied to my back to break my fall whenever I felt like jumping from the top bunk to the bottom bunk, and then down to my flowered-daisy twin bed covered in throw pillows. No idea that the pillowcases tied to my shoulder blades wouldn't help me float. This was the way I felt now, like pillowcases had taken the place of my wings. Like I would never fly despite my attempts. Like an invisible burden was trembling between my heart and thighs.

I followed behind the nurse, trailing after her socks. Argyle. I loved argyle. The pattern had dabs of pink and

4

brown, and it was all a blur as she airily whispered to me as she showed me to the room in the far back. I seemed to be the only patient, although this office had swallowed— my count—four others, and none of them had come out. We got to the room, and I climbed on top of the table, which was too high to reach without using the stool.

"Would you like to hear the heartbeat?" She breathed the words in a faint murmur.

I stared with no response as if I didn't even know what a heartbeat was. I was scheduled for an abortion today; why ever would I want to hear the heartbeat? I wasn't ready for that question, and I wasn't sure she was supposed to ask it. Maybe she was religious, or maybe she saw something in my eyes jumping around the room. I nodded, although I wasn't sure.

I hesitated as I watched my feet sway childlike against the side of the table. The walls seemed to glow white now, so white—you'd think the nurses would have had enough empathy to turn them down. I leaned toward the back of the table. The nurse eased my neck in her hands until I reached the pillow. My chest swelled, and for the millionth time in the last week, I stared at my stomach as if a gargoyle were going to pop out of it right that second.

She covered my jeans with a thin white sheet, a standard procedure among nurses with kind paper smiles and stinky powdered gloves. My breathing sped up, and the wetness under my armpits began to pulse. She tucked my Betty Boop shirt under my breasts, and I helped her hold it up with my hands. I thought she was going to bend over and grab at the ultrasound machine, but instead, she reached over to guide my arms down to both sides.

My fingertips began to ache, eyes involuntarily blinked; my blood was seething beneath my skin. Her motions quickened as she grabbed for a cold gel, and I jumped slightly at the touch of it on my abdomen. Seconds later, a device similar to a high-tech flashlight was sliding around my lower abdomen, pressing inward ever so slightly. It was an ultrasound wand. I looked over at the monitor, at the swirl of mass moving, at the slosh of blah on the screen, at the cluster of what looked to me more like a peek into a tiny version of fuzzy outer space. I stared at the screen as I listened to the fast, faint thrumming, the catastrophic image burning into its own little outer space, strong and growing stronger like fierceness, a tiny hammer beating. Music.

I would never remember anything more than that hesitation, the way I could feel my veins; it was as if they were screaming in a mute moment. Like drowning with my eyes wide open. Death in slow motion. I was thinking about how I'd give my life for this baby, this growing mess of outer worldliness. I was thinking about how not having control over this made me want to cry and run.

How I wished I was in a video game or that I could sleep through this.

It was terror. And then I felt it, like an anxious solitude: Mothers did not do what was best for themselves. Mothers did what was best for their babies. I had the feeling of being a mother.

Tears churned in my eyes, and for those few seconds I was outside of my body, envisioning my child. My doll. My. Mine. I was scheduled to be awake for the abortion the entire time, and this, I assumed, would take place in another room. I was supposed to walk out "me" again; I was supposed to wake up different tomorrow. I would wake up tomorrow without a baby. My baby. My. Mine.

I'd been reading about pregnancy and abortion. I understood the consequences: the bleeding, cramping, and clotting. The process of the suction, the fact of the abortion being twenty-nine times more powerful than a household vacuum cleaner. I knew I was approximately eight to ten weeks pregnant and that right now, my baby had eyelashes and could squint and turn somersaults inside of me. My baby probably had webbed fingers and feet like I'd seen in the pictures I'd seen supporting pro-life, the propaganda advertising bloody burnt-veined corpses online, children that were forced-born, and in overly bold print "LEFT COUNTER SIDE FOR DEATH."

The tiny hammer beating was now more like little men in Timberland boots kicking me in the heart—not because I felt abortion was wrong but because I didn't know what choice was right. I felt out of body, out of mind, and out of touch: insanity only the insane might understand. How insane for that person to be me. I should never have had sex anyway. I'd waited so long to have sex with him because I wanted it to be special. I'd waited exactly one year. I'd waited until he said he was in love with me. I shook my head in my hands.

I sat back on the table and fiddled with the corner of a parenting magazine that sat on the stand nearby. I pictured myself pushing the "rocking" stroller in the advertisement. The nurse turned away.

When I first found out that I was pregnant, I'd gone to my family doctor because I was "stopped up." My constipation had gotten so unbearable that my father had to take me for a checkup. I told the doctor my symptoms and peed in a cup, and he'd sent me home with stool softeners.

When I was a little girl, I'd always had problems with constipation. Ma would tease me, "Ya full of shit, girl!" I squeezed my temples and eyes tightly. I wished she were saying that now and that I was only constipated. Everything used to be better before Mama and Daddy split up. I would have never expected this. I couldn't have

wildly imagined then that I'd be here, staring at the white

buttons on the nurse's coat as she prepared to give me an

abortion. I felt hot tears drowning out my eyes. Far off in

the distance, I heard delicate voices in the hallway begin

to get closer.

My stomach purred in knots, and an intense churning

took over my body. The skin around the nurse's eyes

pinched, she blinked too quickly, and when she breathed

in, it was like she was forcing herself. It was like she was

begging me with her eyes to have my baby. I squeezed

the brown cushion of the table and as she looked at me

again, my body shook hard. She might let me go if I

changed my mind. What if I had this abortion and could never have children again? Dad had already formed his opinion about me—telling him it wouldn't happen again or explaining it was the first time isn't going to matter. Adrenaline was rocking inside me—what if they held me down? What is it going to feel like when I wish I'd had my baby? When my little girl would have been three? When my son would have graduated from fifth grade? The voices increased, and I heard a woman say, "Is she ready?" Fear broke every threshold of every feeling, and I tore away the sheet and felt the discomfort of my shirt falling over my moist stomach and took to running. I ran to the door, door open, hallway, hallway long, emergency exit, emergency exit, lobby, lobby long, big, lost, somebody help me, street—where?

There.

I ran full speed toward the street. Didn't hear anyone follow and didn't hear anyone call my name at all. I ran toward the bus stop. As I ran, I thought, "Well, Ma, I'm definitely not full of shit this time."

Direction didn't come easy to me. I looked around, panic-ridden. I knew I could catch a bus, and I'd always wanted to. I wished Mama and Daddy would have let me ride the bus alone like some of the other teenagers. It occurred to me just then that I'd never been on a bus before because Daddy used to say it wasn't safe. I didn't

know exactly where I was, but I would rather have been

lost than in that clinic. Bamboo grass surrounded the

courtyard. Cars zizzed by. All I wanted was my mommy.

I would run to her and tell her that I was in love and I was

having a baby and I was afraid of everything and

everything would not be ok, but it would be whatever it

would be. Something about knowing a little person was

growing inside of me made me want her, need her,

understand the hopelessness and fanatical helplessness

motherhood must bring. The fear of feeling the

undeniable urge to want to love and protect a tiny doll

and know all at once I needed to still be loved and

protected myself. To know I had forty-six dollars in an

account somewhere and I'd never bought diapers before made me feel hopeless. But someone was going to understand why I wanted to have my baby, and why as impossible and unfortunate as that sounded in the tenth grade, there was still a reason to have my child. I just didn't know what that reason was.

I got on the first bus that slowed at a stop in front of me, a bus that could've been going anywhere. A bus that seemed to come from a whirlwind of places I'd never been. All I knew was that it was going somewhere, and I needed somewhere to go. I knew I was at least thirty to forty minutes from home, and I was in Los Angeles, but where exactly was beyond me. I wanted to reach the

intersection of Rodeo and La Cienega, near Culver City. I
was born and raised in Culver City, but Mama moved out
with my sister into a condominium that sat on that corner
nearby. I wasn't paying attention on the ride there
because Dad hadn't said much to me, and I knew he was
either taking me to somewhere to dump my body or
taking me somewhere to remove my baby. Riding to the
clinic, I couldn't tell which was worse. Now, getting on
the bus for the first time, alone, I begin to wish I'd let him
dump my body.

When the doors opened, shock took hold, and I was
not able to speak. I squeezed the tiny lavender purse
Mama had given me. It was filled with a few items: Lip

Smacker lip glosses, Lifesavers Gummisavers, a journal nearly complete with newly written poetry, a wallet with a few quarters and a twenty-dollar bill. The bus driver had long black extensions with pink accents and a gap between her two front teeth. She stared at me. Her mouth was open as if I'd stolen something or as if I were going to rob her bus even though I was, as my comedic and painfully blunt family doctor put it, "Pregnorant."

At this point, pregnorant was ok for me. Not only because of the good-humored context with which my doctor spoke the word but because pregnancy wouldn't last forever, and ignorance, by definition, meant I was unaware, which could also be a temporary state. What was permanent was motherhood or the act of choosing

not to be a mother. In the middle of this thought, I noticed

passengers were putting their coins and swiping some

type of ticket-like paper, while I walked up to the bus

driver to offer her my twenty.

"Grrrrrl, sit down. If you put that in my machine, you

won't get no change."

I sat in the front and peered out of the window of the

bus, not knowing where it was going. My white shirt was

still wet from the ultrasound gel, and my face felt puffy

with fear and red from running. I couldn't manage a

thank-you, but as we caught eyes, I knew the bus driver

knew I was thankful. Suppose I got off of this bus and

walked into a new life? What if I exited this bus, and no

one was there—only my fall from safety, strangers, and

suffocating disappointment? Tears came silent and heavy,

stomach cramps throbbing through me—I sat in the front

of the bus, squeezed between a lady who looked almost

dead and a spiky-haired teenager with headphones and a

checkered belt. I thought to myself: I've got to keep calm,

or I'll hurt my baby.

The bus slowed, and the time-lapse could have been an

hour or a few minutes. With each stop, my heart raced

until I saw the gas station that never had any change and

the car dealership I'd passed before. I realized I was on

Figueroa near the University of Southern California. This

meant I wasn't too far from home. Home being Culver City, and if we kept going in the same direction, I'd get close. The bus driver turned to me.

"What's yo stop, honey?"

"Keep straight," I breathed, barely audible, as if my tone could dictate the way she was going to drive the bus. I looked over and saw a Latino woman enter the bus with her twin girls. She carried their fold-up stroller as they cooed and touched everything they could reach. They wore matching pastel sundresses and filthy tennis shoes; maybe they were two years old. I watched her struggle to get them on the bus, bumping everyone apologetically. One child was in her arms, the other was grabbing at her jeans' pocket. When the bus screeched to a stop, all of the passengers swayed together in sync. The child she held at her hip put her chin on her mother's shoulder. I thought the greatest comfort in the world was surely the closeness of that love. The baby turned her head sideways and closed her eyes.

I noticed passengers were pulling a string to notify the bus driver of their need to get off. What if all I had to do was pull a string and change the course of my life? What if all I had to do was speak up and say, "I know we talked about the importance of my future and the fact that I want to go to college, Dad, but my baby has a heartbeat. Dad, my baby has a heartbeat already."

I pulled the string. What if getting on this bus was accepting that fate was taking me somewhere? What if I walked off of this bus a mother?

That bus eventually let me off adjacent the entrance of the Carl's Jr., less than a block from Mama's condo. I got off. It was only then that I thought about my dad's feelings. Alone and worried in the lobby, waiting for me to return to comfort me—babyless. I walked into the Carl's Jr., ordered a double cheeseburger, fries, and shake, and barely had enough energy to toss my folded twenty and snatch my change from the counter. I sat in the booth, taking in the fast-food aroma. I stared at the order number on the table. My burger arrived as my

stomach growled loudly. I looked around to see who'd
heard. I was scared and worried about how I could be
someone's mom. Ten weeks pregnant was the best time
to get an abortion, I'd once overheard someone say. Ten
weeks pregnant was also an opportune time to decide to
be a mother. I picked up my burger in both hands, bit into
it, felt the excess grease in the corner of my mouth as I
chewed. Contentment spread across my face, by the
second bite, a lot less fear.

My, weren't my baby and I hungry. My. Mine.

# WISHFUL THINKING

"Made my bed guess I'ma lay in it." Those were his stupid words.

First of all, I didn't make my bed back then, and I didn't live with him, so I wasn't sure if he ever had. But neither one of us needed to *lay* together in the first place because we were just kids, so I was sure there was no way we should've been *laying* anywhere. But he told me this lie after we slept together, so let's start there.

*His words…* meaning, Him #1: the one I had a child with. He was conveniently coined my "baby daddy" by my then-teenage friends. We had nothing else to give each other but time and attention. I don't believe I'd ever stayed on the phone with anyone for as many wee hours in the night as him. It was for sure puppy love; nonetheless, I do love puppies.

Aborting our child would have been too hard for me emotionally. I feared the loss of my baby more than childbirth or motherhood. I'd managed to push out my little banana-colored Dennis The Menace before actually ever having my first orgasm.

I would look at Him #1, Henry, as my train wreck-in-waiting and wonder if he would ever crash into me again. Even back then, my romantic ideals took over my common sense. Truth is. He did. By the time we'd had sex the second time, I was already pregnant with my son; I just didn't know. I had tunnel vision with a side of *why me*.

Henry walked around, much like the world owed him something—the worst case of entitlement I'd ever seen, next to my son's. My son's outlook and demeanor became eerily similar to his dad's attitude, even though I didn't think he spent enough time with him for there to be any learned behavior.

Some endings do more than just hurt you.

They haunt.

# WISHFUL THINKING

TIME IS THE ONLY THING WE *REALLY* HAVE.

My son's father wasn't ever going to change—it would be silly to think it so. I had always known I wouldn't be an exception to this rule. But I still kept getting more creative with the rules and the ways I thought some did and did not apply to me. We never actually "broke up." I just found out I was pregnant and told him, and he never called again.

I saw him in the distance one time long after, as I was dropping off my then-less-than-three-year-old son to spend time with his grandparents. Henry had been in and out of gangs and jail, and I'd heard about it. He was smoking something that looked stuffed with other things, but he also smoked cigarettes—around our son. The only

thing that ever meant anything to me after our breakup
was the image he painted—for our son.

I once heard *the worst sickness is the one you know is
happening, but you can't do anything to stop it.* Children
are impressionable. Anything left unexplained was
subject to their interpretation and, depending on mental
and emotional states of mind, could hit them differently. I
wish back then I'd known this—even more. I was broken,
so I didn't date anyone for a few years after my son was
born. I just read to him, played him music, and wrote
poetry in my journal—but he would still soak up every
influence I tried to keep from him.

Dating had always been uphill with skates for me. Distracting and distracted. Never quite reaching the rainbow—much of the slippery slide, never a pot of gold at the end.

Chuck Palahniuk said, "You're always haunted by the idea you're wasting your life."

Had my life become a waste already? I was a young mother with no love interests. Not sure how to make a living or by doing what. People tend to wish on the things they want. Before they have planned, researched, or scouted potential mentors. Before weighing possible outcomes, we wish on them. So that was what I did.

"Make a wish, baby, make a wish!" I told my son.

Year after year, he made a wish.

Lavish birthday parties I could hardly afford. Over and over. I doted on my son. I dressed him in newsboy hats and plaid ties, colorful moccasins.

He was my center, and for so many years I gave him my wishes. I worked hard to support him. I was just too afraid to wish on anything again.

I attained corporate low-paying jobs until I finally decided to get a degree in management. I took an interest in marketing and advertising.

I could have had a quiet baby, a polite child, a toddler who slept when I slept, and a kid who finished early, first of his class. Instead, my mini did none of the above. He finished his schoolwork whenever he felt like it, better than all of his classmates.

I'd get called about my son sleeping through lectures, head down through group assignments, but his homework was correct—pretty good test scores overall. I couldn't really get upset, but then again, I guess I could.

The day my son told me he no longer wanted to play football, he was in eleventh grade. I'd been paying for football leagues and summer camps for a little under three years. He said for a few years he'd been writing music, and he wanted to rap. I sighed but performed a secret little cheer. I heard his demo and thought: he's going to be a broke little musical genius on my couch forever and ever, *just great.*

On the one hand, it was safer than football, but on the other hand, I knew he was talented. He could write to music. I just had words. That meant a struggle neither one of us could afford.

\*

My mentor and I would often talk in the afternoons. Between work and school, I would pick up my son. She was always so positive; I, however, was not. No matter if

I liked it or not, my choices shaped me. I didn't understand that I could create my world.

She said I had to let go of the idea of it working out. What it used to be and what I thought it would be. She said there were times I had to keep hope, and there were times I needed to make a new wish.

"I don't wish for anything. I haven't made a wish in— I don't know how long," I retorted.

"You are, and you have been, and that's what's so stifling and scary. You're wishing on an outcome. You keep wishing things were different."

I guess, deep down, I was subconsciously rubbing genie lamps and throwing coins in waterfalls and wells, but I kept telling myself the wrong story. I kept thinking someone was going to save me.

## How?

She said, let go of it.

She said, to be in the now.

I said, how, *I love him, how?*

She said, ***there will be a Series of Hims.***

***This was just Him #1.***

I nodded and looked down.

~ ~ ~

"You have to get better at letting go, *better* at letting it go. You cannot move on—holding on," she said again.

I remember closing my eyes—my hands gripping my face.

"Don't you want anything else?" she continued, the sun setting slowly in the background.

Over and over, I used to discuss with her what my friends would tell me about my "baby daddy." The laughingstock I became was heart-wrenching. Some of the things I heard people say about me would wake me out of my sleep with embarrassment and regret.

"A family," I answered her, looking at her without blinking. "I want a family who sits at their kitchen table discussing their day together—a mom, a dad, and a child mumbling and bumbling about nothing."

"Right," she said. "You want what you've never had."

\*

"Your daddy's not comin' home right now, so you might as well getcha lil' ass on up them stairs and go on to bed." Mama was so harsh and sounded even more Southern when she'd been drinking.

I, maybe about eight or nine, sat at the bottom of our swiveled staircase in front of the big screen. Ma would bring me food there, or Maria, the maid, would. Maria lived in the house with us, as she took my sister's room when she moved into our back house with her husband—and what would be their first child. I don't remember ever living in the house with my sister because far back as I can remember, she was already gone. My half sister was from Mama's previous relationship, but we weren't half anything to me.

We never ate at the table. It was always dinner there on the floor or TV trays. Mama would holler into that phone for hours. When my friends came over, we would imitate her, and one even asked if she was deaf—she was so loud. I responded no and explained her voice just carried like that, but I don't think any of my friends believed me. I'd overhear her talk until the cordless phone ran out of battery—curse, then curse again at me to find the other receiver somewhere around the house. Then, she would pick it back up like it hadn't been out at all.

"You still there? Ok, yea babiiie, this chile honey, she sit 'round here all day doin' nothin' and when I ask her for the other phone, she ain't seen it," she'd say, rocking the receiver between her neck and shoulder to get the right angle—continuing on.

It wasn't sadness. It wasn't anger. It was sheer emptiness I would feel. This was the typical evening, and

Daddy was never home early. I would sit in the corner and read. I would sit with my diary or my many journals clutched tight to my chest like the smallest child, saying nothing for hours and hours. The only time Mama ever saw me was when we went shopping. At first, I hated shopping, and then, as I grew older and started to care more about my appearance, I began to look forward to it because it was the only time I felt she actually noticed me. I think, as children, we want most to be seen, and praised, and as adults, that translates to approval and appreciation. But always… and in all ways, we all want—*even just a little bit*—attention.

Daddy would get home, and I would feel him pick me up and fall into his arms even heavier. It would be late, but he would scoop me big and full into his arms and climb around and up to the top of the stairs. The steps would creak even though they had brownish-dull carpet covering them. He'd push the door open with one hand; I'd peek open one eye, then close it, wiggle a bit, then giggle. He'd slide me into my bed next to my pink pig pillow and Gloworm. He'd kiss my forehead and wouldn't say a word; he just knew I was waiting on him.

Childhood imprints don't have to be physical traumas to affect your perspective of the world. I used to believe it had to be something particularly dramatic that had to shape your world. What I've come to find out is that

sometimes the smaller issues become the most severe—as

the more hidden problems can be even harder to figure

out.

No one ever asked me if I was ok after I had a child

and became a teen mom. Once you bring a child into this

world, it becomes about the child and not you. I had to

process the first and only breakup of my life while

watching all of my wishes grow into numb pieces of

dreams. I also had to learn how to be the mom I didn't

know how to be yet. There was no time to figure out who

I'd wanted to be.

I thought as soon as I had my child, I wouldn't crave anything else, but, like anyone else, I would. Depression sank in so deep I couldn't tell if it was day or night.

I used to wonder: Would I die from the loneliness of raising my child alone?

A broken heart?

Surely, it'd be one of the two.

Would I be so preoccupied with my own shortcomings I'd fail to see the next train coming?

I'd lost hope after Henry because being with him was the first time I'd ever really hoped on anyone.

Henry was the person I *attracted* because broken people speak the same broken language, usually. I was a spoiled latchkey child seeking attention. He was a spoiled class clown seeking attention. We were both only children from our parents' other halves—that I knew of. They'd had children from previous relationships who didn't grow up in the same households. He gave me as much attention as I gave him—it was laughter in a type of lovesickness. I think deep down, we were attracted to each other because we could provide each other with what we didn't get enough of at home. Attention.

The reason I knew this was the same reason I'd developed distaste for Henry's parents. When our son was younger, they had a very "*you need us—you little girl*" point of view. I'd asked them for a little help, and they'd resented me for choosing to have Henry's child. Every time I'd pick my son up, he'd be sitting in front of the television. I knew Henry had been raised the same way. I left my son with his grandparents less and less as time went on.

My mentor was right. Henry was just Him #1.

He was the hurt I needed, so I'd be forced to find my focus.

Now the question was, where was I going?

I enrolled in school.

WISHFUL THINKING


I WISHED FOR REAL LOVE.



Wishful Thinking

# CHAPTER 2

# FUCKED

The moment I met Evan (Him #2), I knew we would fuck. We took astrology together; he wanted to study aviation. "Make a wish," he told me in the back seat of his old Camry. Stars dazzled through the open sunroof and then faded away. I wished to be beautiful on nights with no visible moon.

I hadn't dated in years, and I was cautious after Him #1. Evan was straightforward: after his smoke sessions, he'd say really basic shit to me like, "You're a good mother." I'd fall for it all. Marijuana made Evan higher

than planes, and when he came down, he landed in me.

His complexion was cashew colored, and his eyes were

wide and turquoise. One sniff of him was ripe with stale

weed, faint Dove soap, and clout crowded with self-

doubt. Anyone could tell something was off, but there

was so much going on around him. Mornings, I'd pass

him at school, and he was leaning against the balcony—

giddy girls laughing loudly around him. He'd motion for

me to come over without breaking eye contact. I fell for

him the day he exclaimed to his buddies outside of class

that I was a keeper. In the hallway, during our break, I

heard him say, "She gotta nice ass, a pretty smile, and

always come prepared fa' class even if she talk through

it." I felt his friend's eyes on my backside: confirmation he'd been talking about me. "Evan and I," he'd said, "were the two people everyone at school wanted to be." His confidence and Cool Water cologne were like a caffeine shot into each of my fingertips and toes. "Hey, babe." Evan reached for a hug. Moments like those made it seem unlikely I'd ever catch my breath again.

Six months later, he was my boyfriend, and I planned to celebrate with our lovemaking. I'd light the dust-covered candles. Afterward, we'd have Mama's leftover pot roast. Maxwell's neo-soul music would play melodically. Evan told me I was beautiful under moonlight. Stars did somersaults inside of me.

\*

That evening, Evan was hours late to my house without a call. When he finally arrived, he was flighty and sweating. We'd had so many good times, but this time, in particular, it didn't go so well.

He dashed to the bathroom. When I heard the door close, I snatched his phone and checked the calls in his contact list, looking for answers. There was Kailey, Andrea, Crystal, and nine missed calls from me. Evan saw me and rushed out of the bathroom from behind me, his cell phone still burning between my hands. I turned and threw it at his chest as he stepped closer to me.

"What the fuck you in my phone for?" His orange pullover was dirty, and his eyes were bloodshot.

"What the hell is going on?" I wailed.

"None of your fuckin' business." His Timberland boots stomped around the room.

"I've been waiting since eight. Were you wit' Crystal? Kailey?"

He threw me back on the bed, and as I rose he pushed me down again.

"Well, let's just call some o' these hoes an' see, then."

I rocked my head back and forth, pretending I was bolder than I was. He pushed my head into the headboard. My son's pacifier fell off the dresser. I squirmed as he held me down with his forearm across my neck. I kicked him in his shin. His hand reached for his zipper. He slapped open a pocketknife and pressed it against my neck. I gasped. I was sorry then, pinned down, paralyzed in panic. With his other hand, he took his finger straight into my vagina. I screamed, then whispered, "I'm sorry," as the blade cut the side of my cheek, trying to wiggle away. My skirt zipper broke seconds before he began to thrash inside of me. I whimpered; his large hand was over my mouth. My face was turned to the side and smashed into a pillow. I no longer fought back as I stared at the white swirled paint along the walls. Stunned with shock, I shrieked to get air. I shut my eyes. Tears slid back into my hair. Across the room, I stared at my son's crib; the laundry basket with socks Mama tied together for me sat next to it. The carpet needed vacuuming. I wished, at that moment, that I would stop breathing. I looked down, and my thigh was slashed into a deep maroon color. My body shook in uncontrollable heaves. I touched my face.

"Why?" I asked.

"Shit happens." His eyes were wild. The door slammed behind him.

I slid off the corner of the blood-soaked bed and threw

up in the middle of the carpet. The smell of my blood

forced me to throw up again. I crawled to the bathroom

and ran only hot water. Pulling myself up, I stepped into

the bath, one leg over as it shook. My head leaned against

the basin. I added cold water and closed my eyes. When I

opened them, the tub water was stained crimson. I sobbed

for Mama, forgetting she was drunk with her friends,

miles away. I wrapped a towel around myself and limped

to my bed. I slid the bloody blanket over me.

\*

Mama came home two days after I'd washed the

covers three times. I never told anyone. Evan was never

seen in class after that. Our astrology professor told me,

"Evan's mother had passed away." I called until one

day—his phone was disconnected. I couldn't believe it. I

wanted him to call me beautiful again.

# FEAR

I once caught a glimpse of Him #2 at Blockbuster

years after the ordeal, and he took off faster than I could

find another breathing soul to tell. I continued to process

negative things that happened to me by pretending they

didn't happen.

<u>everything's ok and fine and all right and mediocre and
hopeless but there's hope in there</u>

Everything's ok. Everything's all right and amazing and
mediocre, and being an open book perhaps has fewer
benefits than I thought. Nonetheless, I'm unchanging.
The wants are catching up with the needs and the maybes.
I'm wondering if cough drops expire. Tired. Every day is
different. Today I'm whining. Nothing has good timing
and the cop, he was blind as batshit, I wasn't speeding, I
was flying.

And everything's fine. Did homework, minded my
business high and mightily, got to work on time. Rent is
paid. Dishes aren't washed, but they're in the water.
Needs don't love me for me. My love doesn't know how
to love me. There's always a chalky aftertaste. The teapot
whistles my favorite song. Acoustic, of course. Smiles
melt a snow cone in yellow, an un-shining yellow. I've

replaced one vice for another. People aren't lovely or wonderful.

There's regret, but that's behind me. Everyone's sleeping with everyone. I'm alone when I'm faithful and grounded. Want a little much, not settling for any. Don't need expensive love—but—finding it hard to zirconia my boots with pennies. None of it makes sense, none of it makes sense. The world doesn't owe anyone shit. That is the part we forget. The part we forget is. Everything's ok. Everything's shining solitaires. Life is shorter than I need reminding of.

Debt is the devil and sacrifice—his midget cousin. Up half the night with worry, most of the day in rush. Somebody's laughter is wizardry. I think I've sunk. Would still have fallen in lovely if he wasn't drunken. So I drowse. Sometimes I wish I could go back—make different choices for you. Sometimes I wished I could go back—make different choices for us. Honey on a paper cut. Sock drawer dreams. There was no reason we couldn't have agreed to disagree, somewhat. For once.

The orchids are menstruating. Like, really, breathing hard. The buoy is shrinking. Butter-byes balance on the balcony. The book closes itself, pats my back to sleep. There's a sixth sense, but the deity missed me. And now it's all happened, life and happenstance. Life and magic brooms. Life in no specific plan or pattern and it's all ok and fine and all right and mediocre and everything's ok and fine and all right and mediocre and hopeless but there's hope in there. Right?

My psych doctor had given me an assignment and told me two things I'll never forget. List your needs; then list your wants.

# FEAR

*The list of what you want was your "why," and if you woke up and did things that helped you to get closer to what's on that list, you'd reach your absolute happiest, you'd find purpose.*

<u>WANTS</u>

1. TIME FOR CREATIVITY + SELF

2. FREEDOM TO EXPLORE

3. INSPIRE + HELP OTHERS

4. NOT WORRY ALL THE TIME

5. FEEL ACCOMPLISHED

NEEDS

1. AIR

2. WATER

3. FOOD

4. HEALTH

5. FAMILY

*She told me that love was already an absolute and happened when your wants met your needs.*

Love—what I thought I'd needed most—didn't even make my list. This work was all internal.

Meagan and I, my old psychologist, worked together for two years after Him #2 (my beautiful blue-eyed boyfriend) raped me in my own bed.

She was blond and thin and mostly wore what I remember as jeans and a nice patterned blouse to our sessions. Those sessions ended up being so hard for me to get through that the woman could have quite possibly worn slacks and a blazer for all I'd know—my eyes were always red and watery. What mattered was that she spoke softly—kind and slow. I spoke fast, always have. I'd found her through the process of looking up people who would accept my insurance. Remembering this process, I still find it rather grueling and by the time you reach someone who could potentially help, you've likely given up hope your problems could be fixed at all, or you've withdrawn back into believing that perhaps there was no problem, which, I've come to find means there was, most definitely, a problem. *Find someone anyway.*

Meagan had what I remembered as blue eyes, and her room had light and dark brown accents, nonmatching furniture, and a brown couch with throw pillows in darker blues. Dimly lit. At that time, I did not believe in talking through my problems. Today, I don't think there are many other ways to self-realization.

In our first sessions, she got to know me through a series of questions about my past. These questions were "the interview," but we flowed like old sisters. As I spoke out loud, I was already speaking similarities of who I was then, and who I'd become. I'd read once that déjà vu meant "you were in the right place at the right time; *keep going*," but I'd also read it could be linked to lack of sleep and anxiety. I felt like I'd have regular bouts of déjà vu just being in the same room with her.

During our next few sessions, I told her I was exhausted and having trouble sleeping because of nightmares and thoughts. A tear slipped down salty onto my lips, then my chin.

"The part you don't understand is the part that angers me most, and it's because I don't know why. I saw him in Blockbuster, and he ran. I'm not sure I can keep going."

She was silent for a bit; then, she looked right through me like she could see the window behind me and said,

"My husband cheated and gave me two STDs, one incurable and one that caused me to lose my child. I'm in physical pain daily, and that will never go away—*you can keep going.*"

I'm sure she wasn't supposed to share any of her personal information with me. That session changed my life in many ways. She made me believe I could keep going, but she hadn't taught me to fight through it, or to

use the pain and change it. That was our last session.

# FEAR

"BOTH OF THE TIMES I CAME CLOSE TO DROWNING, I WAS WITH MY FATHER. THE FIRST TIME, THE BOAT FLIPPED OVER AND A ROPE CAUGHT MY FOOT. FOR A FEW SECONDS I WAS HELD UNDER IN A TANGLE OF PANIC AND METAL AND ROPE. WHEN I CAME UP, NO ONE HAD NOTICED AND I NEVER MENTIONED IT."

- EULA BISS

I'd drowned, but since no one noticed and no one knew, I made no mention. I never saw being raped as something I needed to heal from. I wasn't there yet.

I didn't get an STD, and it didn't result in a child.

There was no need to tell anyone.

But then things started to happen. I developed an obsession with watching *Law & Order: Special Victims Unit*, and I felt like crime television and teary eyes were enough to fix everything. Mariska Hargitay was going to show up any day now, any day. I didn't say anything to anyone because my problems had been compared with a seemingly more significant problem. What was clear to me now, in this finite world, was that what happened to me did not matter. It had to go away. I put it away.

The more I decided nothing happened to me, the more anxious I got. I'd mastered moving on, but I never mastered healing. I picked my cuticles until they bled. I shook my leg uncontrollably. Because I'd hidden so much of me, I wanted to be seen—even more. I got really good at being what I called an open book private person.

I kept waiting for someone to notice I was broken, for someone to save me from something they couldn't see. The problem was, when someone finally saw me, took interest enough to ask me questions and feel my answers… I reverted back to not wanting to be seen.

I ran. I hid. I downplayed my dreams. I told myself they weren't possible because I felt unlucky. I'd gotten beyond it not being my fault, but I couldn't form a trusting relationship or many friendships at all.

Anyone close to me was cut off, and if they somehow infiltrated the system, I was needy and insecure. Some days, I would look off into a distance for hours. Day after day, I would drive the same area and somehow still I got lost.

*

When I was a child, Mama would make chicken for dinner, and there'd be a real wishbone. She'd ask me to hold it and make a wish over it. We'd both pull gently, and whoever ended up with the largest side of the wishbone was supposed to get their wish. I always got the larger one, but none of my wishes ever came true.

And then I met Liam, who really was everything I'd ever wished for…

# CHAPTER 3

# HOPELESS

In the beginning, Him #3 used to buy me flowers. I would usually smash the dried flowers between my notebook pages. Next time a man buys me flowers—I promised myself—I'd place them in one of my artsy vases, the ones I kept empty. I'd make sure I watered them and that they got light from the sun. I'd make sure I enjoyed their bloom instead of just looking up one day and seeing they were dead. All I was doing was waiting. Wishing. Wishing I had wings, wishing I were living a different life. Wishing… I could fly. Wishing I could

change lives, wishing I could change mine.

We met at the gym. I worked the front desk but was

eventually promoted to sales, and then the membership

retention department. It was surprising how many people

would ask me how much I liked "selling people a dream,"

implying most would never lose weight or get toned at

all. I believed I let people sell themselves their own

dream, and I was only there to show them a cool place to

work out while they did so. After months of walking into

the gym and flirting with me, Him #3 came right up to the

front desk and sold me my very own dream. It was on the

back of a guest pass that had my name misspelled across

the front. In it: a drawing. A scribbled heart with a face
and a note that read,

"Was looking forward to seeing your smile today ☺" –

Liam

He thought I wasn't at work.

I'd always written poetry, but after Liam, I started
telling stories.

When I came back from the bathroom and saw the
note, my face beamed and blushed warm, my cheeks
pink. I didn't have to think for a second who the note was
from. The dapper stranger with dark hair and bushy

eyebrows and a solid yet slender build. He was milk chocolate with Tarzan shoulder blades and an "I have candy" smile. He came to work out in the evenings— unwinding my breath when he opened the door like some nostalgic old novel with the pages flittering about so much you'd have to hold them down.

For a few years, we dated, and eventually, we moved in together. That was when things changed rapidly. Liam was excessive about where things went and insisted on things happening only his way. It started with just small disagreements until I got accustomed to giving him his way to avoid the trouble. He learned he could control me in that way. If ever he couldn't, he'd resort to doing something *really* crazy. He once cut up every skirt I owned and placed them neatly back into their respective places in my dresser. Another time he found my personal diary and started reciting it out loud to me.

I stopped writing those stories and went back to poems I never had to confirm nor deny.

He drank and became several different people: Some of those people were mentally, emotionally, or physically abusive. All of those people were killing me. Most of those people were remorseful. Some of me believed he was sorry. All of me was fearful. Most of me loved him anyway.

## Jump In the Water

he said i love you once—indirectly because of it,

i grew a peach in my heartbeat instantly—the day
blurred.

he said jump in the water baby jump in the water

after you do it, write it, call me back tomorrow

and giggle and read through every line in my center

and listen to it falling like glitter and glasses

and listen to it growing like mastering your craftiness

and i did, I DID, like a big girl

and it was cold and colder and the color of a coma

and it was cold and no one was there.

guess what he's gone

and there goes my hope and my prayer

some days are harder, like there's no God even there

some days i'm reckless and never-y,

some days i'm really "picturing us together"

and what better to hang me by my own diving?

spoiled me with attention and timing

his thoughtfulness made me fall inside myself


jump in the water baby jump in the water

well i can't; it's too deep; I'll sink in his dream:

well i don't dream, anymore.


jump in the water baby [he said] jump in the water

he said—you know,

you are everything i ever wanted from a flower.


What good would it do? What good was having a

dream if fear weighed so much more? When I'd jumped

and fallen. My fears planted themselves there and grew.

Could I have caught my trigger points early enough? To what, calm myself down? Learn more about self-care techniques? Were those the only defenses against love turned inside out?

*

I was in my second year of community college, and I was trying to figure out what I wanted to do and who I wanted to be. I stayed late after class often; I was one of *those* learners. It wasn't just school to me if I was challenged to think, process, and create solutions. It was mandatory. I took a psychology class, and the teacher was rooted in the wildest philosophies. I took to him instantly. I wish I could remember his name, but it was so many years ago. Old and short with all-white hair—balding but holding to what was left of it. He walked with a slight limp and should have had a cane. One day, I asked him a personal question.

"Why do you think someone who'd been so good to me would become someone so bad for me?"

I knew he'd have an interesting answer; we often debated in class. I could always tell from his eye contact that he wanted me to get as much from the class as possible—he always gave me a love analogy—when he'd address everyone else with a less complicated life-related analogy.

He looked down, then back up, then smirked and said:

"Good parenting is rare.

Learning from mistakes is hard.

It's all in the application."

Every afternoon after that, I made sure I was there asking him questions about life, about love, soaking up his thoughts about staying away from what he coined as *lovers who were only after what they could get from you*. I wanted to study relationships, and I loved learning about how to see the signs in life and love. We are all projects.

He started reading my poems; he told me I was a good storyteller and that he could hear the stories in them. The more I'd write, the more he'd read. When I would leave, he would tell me he couldn't wait to hear next week's.

Him #3 said his parents broke up when he was just a young boy—his mom raised him and his twin sister. When I asked about his dad, his words verbatim were, "The only time I wanna see him is when he is kissing my ass and I'm face-down in a casket." Apparently, his father was abusive.

My psychology teacher had been right: in order for me to love the right person, I had to understand and spot early-on *how* to know if someone had really learned from their previous selves, and how, *and if*, they'd actually reinvented themselves as new people, which for most was tricky, if not almost impossible.

When someone has dealt with emotional, mental, or physical trauma, it's the same healing process as an illness, an addiction, or a loss… a long process such as therapy always is. They must show they've rehabilitated. That person must live in that new space, and that must become who he or she is now. Him #3 couldn't admit he had any problem and definitely wouldn't apply anything he hadn't learned from any problem of his that didn't exist to his knowledge.

I could say I learned *how* to learn from that teacher, but what was more important was that I learned why it was essential to keep learning. It was imperative even if for no other reason than to learn how to, one day… save myself.

But, I guess then, the problem… was in the application.

\*\*\*

When I was drowning, I thought about a few things: Pastel butterflies, blowing dandelions, dreamcatchers—or were they spider webs? Faeries, or rather, their wings.

On one of Liam's drunk nights, I woke up, body slanted with my bare face on the concrete of some stranger's driveway. I had a bloody nose, and my clothes were torn. All I could remember was that he'd left me. I hadn't been drinking. The sun was bright and gave me a headache right through my squinted eyes.

But my heart—oh my heart—I promise hurt worse.

# HOPELESS

IMBALANCED RAINBOWS MAKE
BEAUTIFUL SKIES. I DON'T REMEMBER ANY
OF THEM.

The thing about pain is, the second you choose to help someone else, your own pain lessens. It's a level-up from distraction by way of transferring your healing energy— then, you receive only what's left, which was maybe only a little less, but as we know, any bit of pain we can lessen is worth an attempt.

So while I was drowning, I kept reaching to save someone else. *At least I could imagine it:*

Avert mission heartbroken—to me as a flying faerie Santa, except instead of delivering Christmas gifts, I'd randomly fly by houses and blow kisses and grant wishes like this:

"Oh, you have cancer? * *Kiss* * It's gone!

"Oh, your husband died? * *Kiss Smaaaaack.* * No longer! Look, he's in the kitchen baking macadamia nut cookies.

"Oh, your mind is broken? * *KissssssssGlitter* * everywhere. Here is the power to heal yourself, you know, just in case it happens again, and I'm not here."

I'd ride off to the next house on that little white Luckdragon Falkor in *The Neverending Story*. I told one of my best friends about these ridiculous delusions, arms flailing in the air like a small child who still believed in magic. I remember she just looked at me—her eyebrow raised up to one side.

"So you some type of light-skinned Tinkerbell from the clouds delivering make-believe dreams like a frou-frou Jesus?"

"Nah, I mean, maybe I'll just inspire people," I said to her.

"You already do," she said. "Just do that."

\*

Mostly he'd just "work late…"

# HOPELESS

ALONE IS LONELY IF YOU LEAVE IT LONG

ENOUGH.

Liam would always return in a rage tantrum after too many swigs. I'd learned; I just had to wait it out until he calmed down. Before I could figure a way to swim out of my lake of tears, he'd have me cloud surfing atop my favorite down comforter.

He was so soft when he wanted to be, but he could turn this part off and become so mean. Sometimes, he'd kiss me everywhere, and I'd be inside a bubble. I'd be nearing my orgasm, and I'd feel him abruptly slide out of me, get up, and walk off. My leg would still be shaking. I would sit up, trying to figure out what I'd done wrong, and there would be an hour or so of silence. He'd become that different person, just right then, at that moment.

Him #3 would regularly give me overdoses of him.

We'd stay locked in the house for days—there were no hours. My love language was always quality time.

Then, like the genie that came only once for my one wish, he'd disappear right in front of my eyes. I'd beg him to come back because I made a mistake and I needed to change my wish, or at least make it more specific, but it was too late. He was gone.

A friend of mine finally proposed to the woman he'd dated for eleven years; she was a writer, so we'd hit it off. I'd invited him and his new almost-wife over for wine and my poor little excuse for a dinner party on my artsy too-small dining table adjacent downtown Culver City—right across from a small area nicknamed Helms Bakery.

I remember looking at them both in the low light of my cheap Ikea setup. The glow she had—the ring blaring on her finger—seemed it was all I saw. We played a game that involved debating specific topics… infidelity came up.

"A person will always only ever be as faithful as his or her options!" my friend exclaimed boisterously.

A year after they married, he got promoted and left her for a singer who made three times as much. Because they'd been amicable and had children together, he'd invited his writerly ex to his wedding. I went. As we sipped champagne, his ex told me she'd calmly whispered to the singer at her reception that, "A person will only ever be as faithful as his or her options."

They divorced three years later. When I asked my friend why, he shook his head, shrugged his arms up, and told me that she'd clearly "found a better option."

## JUMP

I still believed in the fairy tale despite everything I saw, felt, and heard. I kept fluffing my then-almost-fiancé's pillows. I kept buying new comforters for our apartment together. Over and over. Modern quilts and new pillows—in different colors and textures, softer, more, and more. I went broke, making our space more comfortable. I couldn't stop *trying* to make it better. This was my way of fixing what I could. I hadn't figured it out yet, but you can't *buy it better.*

*

I grew up in a household where everything appeared "fine." I learned to pretend everything *was* fine. When I used to get home from school, Mama had already folded or flip-tied my socks, and they were always sitting on my bed waiting for me to put them away. She did things like this to make up for me being latchkey, so mostly that meant she wasn't going to be home. I could do what I wanted: I could have my neighbor-friend Kelly over without asking. We could make syrup-and-bread sandwiches and sit on the roof until it got too cold. No one would miss us or know we were there at all.

In the evenings when I finally heard Mama stumble in, bags were shuffling—she'd been shopping. I listened for her slur—she'd been drinking.

Mama always meant so well; she showed it in the food she fixed, the places she took me, or wherever she dropped me off. Sometimes just in the way she warned what not to do so I didn't get hurt or die. There was very little she did *for* fun, and there was nothing we ever really *shared* as commonalities but a roof.

Few things make a person only temporarily happy faster than shopping and drinking. In Mama's case, she'd continue drinking through the night—so there wasn't a down. She didn't view Daddy's money spent as a loss for her—yet another up. Mama used to take me to Fedco (let's just say it was the old Target for lack of explanation), and she'd get me something to "spruce up" my room or the house, or an outfit. It was her way of putting things back together. I, however, went for a new comforter. Some softer something-or-other that I thought would make my life better in the form of an egg crate or new pillow. I'd learned this from Mama. Now, when I started fluffing pillows... it was time to have a sit-down.

Probably, the pillows were fine.

It was always me who was not.

LIFE IS UNFAIR

WITH A SIDE OF FUCKED UP

AND WHEN PEOPLE SAY GOOD LUCK

WHAT THEY REALLY MEAN IS

"I HOPE YOU'VE TRAINED HARD ENOUGH

TO BALANCE EVERYTHING ON YOUR

PLATE."

The year before I got pregnant, Daddy hired a private investigator to follow Mama around and confirm his suspicions of her infidelity. At that time, Daddy was losing the house I'd grown up in. He managed to buy another one not too far from it that next year, but things in the new house were never the same. We all moved there, but all of us never really *lived* in that house together—we were all different parts of our old selves, *dying*.

When he used to tell me about it, after I was older and mature enough, and mostly when I'd talk to him about Liam's cheating ways, he'd say stuff like, "If your mama had just admitted she was wrong, we could've gotten

through it," and, "She never really said she was sorry."
He'd said that when he confronted her about seeing
someone else and told her he had the pictures of her
coming out of a hotel, she'd said to him, "Shit happens,"
and then threw her hands up in the air.

Shit didn't *just happen*. A person had to *make* or *let*
shit happen, which was proof we had some control and
choice in how things could turn out. Also, her sorry
wouldn't have meant much to him; he wasn't very
forgiving, and he focused on blaming her for what
happened, not finding out why it happened.

JUMP


SOME OF YOUR DISHES ARE GONNA FALL

AND BREAK.


OK?

I couldn't imagine an early thirties guy like Him #3, dapper as ever, would go from working at a sports store to the airport, and then finally fulfilling his dreams of becoming a DEA officer only to revel in the options his new paycheck afforded him. I just didn't think he would cheat.

I thought he'd be more grounded. Our relationship felt so stable—the way he'd hold my face in both hands, the way he'd stand in the doorway admiring me. But in fact, it was everything but stable.

JUMP

WHAT REALLY HAPPENED NEVER MATTERS:

THE ONLY THING THAT MATTERS

IS WHAT THE PERSON YOU LOVE THINKS

HAPPENED.

He celebrated his narcissism-kissed arrogance. He continued to display signs of multiple personality disorder, according to everything I'd started to learn of it, and it scared me.

I stopped studying psychology.

I dropped out of school entirely.

# JUMP

A PERSON MAKES TIME FOR WHO AND WHAT

HE OR SHE WANTS.

THIS IS NOT NEGOTIABLE.

One of my first mentors answered my phone call—midspeech at a podium—and explained to the audience that I was "going through something," and he simply "had to answer."

My bestie would even answer my phone call when she said she was showering. I'd interrupt her,

"Wait-wait, so you have soap on you? Why did you even pick up?"

"Well… can I just give you a call back later? I just wanted to know if it was important."

I began to equate this particular "busy" excuse with a liar, someone I couldn't trust, because in my experience, that's all it had been when people told me they were

busy. It got harder for me to understand, "I'm busy; I'm

working." It became a trigger for me despite what might

have actually happened, no matter how real or imagined.

Busy with work was an excuse to me. No one was ever

*too busy* with work, it was never *too complicated*, and no

one could ever be *too distracted*. It just meant the person

was too preoccupied with what mattered more.

The woman my then-fiancé cheated with was the

daughter of his mother's boyfriend. I'd seen her before,

actually, at a gathering. Many times, I'd been accused of

things I'd had valid reasons for, but after his storytelling,

I found reasons equivalent to excuses. Nobody was

actually "too busy" or "busy with work." They just made the choices they wanted to make. Giving people reasons was like stating a case you'd usually already lost. What never matters is what you say; what matters is if they believe you.

JUMP

IF SOMEONE WANTS YOU, THAT PERSON
WILL ALWAYS MAKE TIME FOR YOU,
OR YOU SHOULD CONSIDER HOW MUCH OF A
SACRIFICE WAITING WILL COST YOU.

Ultimately, I'd just been lied to.

I started to question him, and as per usual, people adapt.

I started to ask more questions. The way he began to set up his lies was so precise—I was shocked. He would go into great detail about the particular way the day was thrown at him, forcing him to detour into some other explanation, but never what I'd actually asked, which was, "How are you?"

I started believing more in the reason I was given a story, rather than how accurate the stories he told were.

If the adage that "time is how you spend your love" is true, then when Liam no longer had quality time, the reasons he couldn't find the time stopped being as important. I'd spent those six years hoping and wishing it wasn't all for nothing.

My closure was in knowing something else was more important to him. I had to stop looking for the "why" Daddy never looked for.

I nervously circled our house, littering the room with white sage spray, lighting incense and candles, and rubbing myself in calming oils. I bit my bottom lip to bleeding. Tears dried on my cheek line as my chest continued to heave. Shock had a way of showing up late to the party after you've unpacked and started to accept it all.

I taught myself how to be ok alone:

How to not need anyone.

How to expect little of everyone, if ever anything.

I conditioned myself to take up the smallest space possible. Hide.

How to take the path with the least resistance to ensure I got by.

# JUMP

NEVER EVER ABOVE ANYTHING. GET YOUR

HOPES TOO *FAR STUCK*

UNLESS YOU ARE BALANCED ENOUGH TO

FALL AND GET BACK UP.

Liam would walk around our house in his "wifebeater" ribbed T-shirt and perfect abs. His ab muscles pulsed through his shirt. He'd flash a smile—I'd coil into laughter, and I wasn't sure what for.

Everything that hurt most about him was because I'd expected him to have some consistency in the effort he made to me. His mind-set and casual natures weren't stable enough to do so.

I wanted to make him happy, even at the expense of my happiness, because I didn't want to say I'd failed. I didn't want to say I still wasn't married. I hated to admit I had been engaged, and it just didn't work out.

It was like I was in this pretty castle of a house we'd built up together, and all I kept thinking was that I was trapped. This... was where he belonged.

I BELONGED SOMEWHERE ELSE.

<u>                            space</u>

Jump roping over broken birdcages I

more than hope about you,

I had to put you in a poem.


I

    had

        to

           *


           (call you)

I just wanted you to love me—flat rate


You are thorough-paced,

Please have mercy on my second thoughts

I had to use all the _____ space.

Sometimes you find the right person in the wrong headspace.

Sometimes you've read the same book but can't find the same understanding.

Sometimes you find yourself when you're looking for someone else.

## Jump Out the Window

Trying to forget you is driving the wrong way on the freeway. So I park.

Negotiating with the rainbow the years go blurry...

Mondays you were fine. But Saturdays you evolved. By evening, you could spread multiple personality disorder to continents on reverse planets. Using "clear water," as you wish it was called, you would have accumulated two domestic violence charges, peed on the floor of your car, and developed a cough.

When you walk in, the walls begin sweating you off.

"Where's the window?" I'm jumping out.

Your justification is a stepstool to a balcony with a
cesspool of warm tropical doubt. Tulips grow from your
lashes and handsome seeps from your mouth in a ticklish
slur. I do nothing but nod in know-all. Suppose.

Suppose respect came in the form of pepper? I would
gussy up your rice, you'd sneeze with appreciation. Our
dinners would pretend for themselves… skylights,
inquisitive statements. Peering over the peas would be,
dare I notice but, flirting, is that you? Rage roared so loud
in chaos and interruption.

The lamp slams me into a whimper, the mirror crushes
into mad lightning in your forearm. Swish and I'm

yelling into the floor: How do I know who you are, how do I know who you are?

And then comes Sunday. Our syllables are soft and dehydrated, and everything's all my fault. Your throat smells impossible. But baby steps, baby steps, and a warm towel. By evening you're making dandelion-shaped teardrops evaporate out of my blouse. And we are now on the other side of the mountain bandaging your hand with gauze.

Streaming red and white sparkling car lights adjusting to a dark navy skyline with stars now pretending they are real slowly coming into focus. Three swift knocks to my foggy tinted window. This really isn't like me, officer, I swear, waking up like this on the side of the highway.

A week after our last bad argument landed me with a bloody lip and a swollen forehead—waking up on some stranger's driveway down Pacific Coast Highway somewhere—I had to do something.

I ran to the park nearest my house. There was a mountain with smaller hills around, but above it—a baseball field. Adjacent the field and more hills, there were picnic tables and a sandy area with a jungle gym and a slide.

*What if no one ever loved me as much?*

*What if I never found anyone who accepted my child and me ever again?*

It was early; no one was there.

I sat with my legs dangling at the browning grassy edge of the mountain, water filling my eyes, trying to imagine who would miss me. The only reason I didn't jump was that the second I got up the nerve, I'd slipped backward and almost fell off the cliff. I stepped back to the green part of the grass—heartbeat pounding in my ears. Thinking and doing were two very different things.

Very.

# CHAPTER 4
# THE PROCESS

**MAMA:** HOW MUCH FUCKIN' PROOF YOU NEED?

**ME:** 90 PROOF APPARENTLY. CÎROC. 5 TIMES DISTILLED. PEACH. FROM THE FINEST GRAPES. THE BOTTLE SAID.

\*\*\*

Eventually (my then-fiancé, Him #3) had an "I Love You" that got his side chick pregnant in a Jacuzzi. How do I know, you ask? Because he told me so. His words were muffled like we were underwater. I was drowning in slow motion.

\*\*\*

I came home one day, and Liam was hiding under the planks that held the mattress. I'd written a poem and called a friend on the phone to recite it, intending to later perform it live. I was saying a bunch of punchy lines about him that I would never say to his face, and I'd gotten about halfway when he popped up angrily, grabbed me by the neck, and shook me; in my fear, I bumped myself into the wall. After I'd hit my head, I then ran toward the door to get out. I smashed a lamp into his shoulder as I scrambled to get to the bathroom. I locked myself in and began heaving. I heard him split his fist through the sliding mirror as he sat in our bedroom, breathing heavy. About ten minutes later, he started banging on the door, begging me to take him to the hospital. As he was asking, his voice began to slur, so I opened up the door. He was losing blood and getting dizzy. I took him to the emergency room, where we found out he needed thirteen stitches across his hand—the most blood I'd ever seen in my life.

\*

*Flashback in a flashback:* the night he'd proposed, I rubbed the scar across his hand as I shook my head in a slow no and simultaneously mouthed the word yes. I was too afraid to say no. When we were intimate, I would think about how charming he was and how no one would believe me if I told them he was killing me—mostly emotionally, but through and through, nonetheless. I thought a few times I'd woken up dead and then realized how ridiculous the thought was.

He would cum inside of me, and I would hope I wouldn't get pregnant. He'd hidden my birth control pills atop the cabinet, too high for me to reach. I'd found them one day as I was cleaning. I realized I hadn't been taking them, but this wasn't the first time they'd disappeared. I stared at the little off-white pill compact...

One time, we'd gotten into an argument because I'd forgotten to chop up the onions to top off his chili. I laughed it off, explaining I had them and would quickly cut them up—they were just in the fridge. He ranted on about his chili getting cold by that time. What I thought a small issue became an ordeal.

"Fix my chili, bitch!" he'd huffed.

My fear resulted in more tears than the onions could ever make as I struggled to cut and mix the green and white onions to his liking. I walked over to scrape the onions from the cutting board. I pushed them with the side of the knife into his bowl. He was disgusted with me, and his breath reeked like an alcoholic torrential storm. He sensed my fear, and it fed him. I hurried from the dining table to the kitchen, and when I saw him coming, I opened the refrigerator door as a divider. When he reached around it at me, my fear grabbed the squeeze bottle of ketchup. Before I knew it, there was ketchup sprayed everywhere. I literally squeezed it and spun around, holding the bottle until it emptied. Our all-white kitchen was a bloody mary mess in less than three minutes. His eyes flared at me, and he was cursing. I picked up the Windex bottle. When he came at me this time, he stumbled, and I let loose on the Windex trigger right into his eyes. He stammered and ran to the bathroom. My chest went up and down heavily; I was breathing through my nose in anger.

I wasn't sure what I was even thinking. I wasn't reacting—I was surviving. I grabbed a knife from the kitchen drawer, convinced that once he could see me, he'd hit me. When I'd found my keys, I ran to the door and saw his Air Force One tennis shoes sitting there. I took the serrated blade of the knife and cut around the edges of his shoes, tracing the line separating the sole of the shoe from the base and tongue. I placed the shoes neatly back against the wall as they were. I hit the driveway, barefoot, my tiny crossbody purse flinging against my back, a knife in one hand, and my car keys in the other. My whole body pulsed. When I reached the door of my car, I saw him at the side of the house, trying to come after me, but he'd attempted to put on his shoes. I saw the Air Forces—they were like two bracelets flinging around, stuck at his ankles. I could see his disgust as his bare feet hit the pavement.

"I'm gonna fuck you up! I'm gonna really fuck you up!" he screamed from the driveway as I was pulling out. A few moments later, I pulled up to my dad's house and

was banging at his door, forgetting I owned a spare key.
Dad opened up, and I saw him band his face wrench
together. He thought I was covered in blood.

When I saw Dad's reaction, I explained to him,
screaming into his face once and again for him to
understand, waiting for what he'd heard me say and what
he saw to register. I was ok, I wasn't bleeding, but I was
covered in dark burgundy ketchup stains, and I had no
shoes on like I'd walked right off the set of a horror
movie. He then grabbed my shoulder and ushered me into
the house. He walked to the hallway and again, back to
the living room, and he draped a blanket over me. I began
at the chili story and ended with Liam and I being still in

love, whispering as if I were convincing myself the most. I reminded him of what Liam said to me just days before, when we were talking about the babies we'd wanted to have.

"I wish you'd have *twins*, it *runs in my family*," Liam had said, the words echoing into me. He'd wished for two of him to go inside of me and for us to be a *family*. This had to have been his third or fourth serious request.

"*Twins*," I repeated back to my expressionless dad.

\*

It stung to find my birth control pills atop that cabinet, but what hurt more was the fact that deep down, I knew Liam had put them there. The stinging clung to my body like poison in my bloodstream. I slept next to him that night without saying a thing. Me missing pills would happen on so many occasions it was pointless to try and keep track of, and random days I'd just start bleeding. My birth control method was prayer.

**BEST FRIEND VIA TEXT MESSAGE AFTER SHE HEARD OUR WEDDING WAS CALLED OFF:**

**BEST FRIEND:** WHERE YOU AT? I WENT STRAIGHT TO VOICEMAIL.

**ME [MUFFLED UNDER A SNIFFLE]:** DROWNING.

**BEST FRIEND:** IN THE BATHTUB?

**ME:** NO. IN THE BOTTLE.

I didn't know how I could love a person I'd feared, but I did. I remember wishing that if I ever fell in love again, I'd want to find someone who didn't drink or who had extreme control far before their limit. Maybe a glass of champagne. A sip here or there. I'd want someone who didn't drink to excess. Someone I always felt safe around.

I'd want to whisper in that person's ear so he could fix whatever issue we ever had long before it became one of those festering issues. I'd him to want to kiss the outside of the Band-Aid after making it feel better. But that idea, it wasn't realistic, at least not without very detailed conversation. Somehow the people I attracted always had communication deficiencies.

Or was it me who had the communication issues?

I always shied away from telling someone when they'd made me unhappy. I'd learned, primarily, how to be afraid to tell the truth about any less-than-favorable situation.

## Because There Is so Much to Say about Falling Apart

I sleep after being with you.

After I wake up

I realize

I do not sleep the same when

I have not been with you.

I do not sleep the same after

I have been around other people.


The laundry dirties itself.

Lies make love to me, then never call.

Looped as ever.

# THE PROCESS

Caught a falling star,

picked up a pencil,

slept through a nightmare with you next to me.


Or was it a falling star I dropped?

Either way or not

I've written it all out.


I've called over the clouds in time for dinner tears,

like a butterfly glazed in a chocolate yes

awfully melting.


You are a flying bruise

come to find me

soaking in Epsom salt and honey.

IT CONSUMES YOU, OR YOU CONSUME

IT. EVERYTHING YOU EXPERIENCE HAS

AN EFFECT ON HOW WELL YOU LIVE.

I moved out one day while Liam was at work. The whole time, all I thought about was how I was going to get away if he'd come home early and saw our refrigerator and couch and everything packed in the back of the moving truck. His car turned the corner just as we were pulling out. He didn't notice, but a few minutes later, my phone started.

The guy I hired to drive the truck looked over at me; both of my legs shook, jiggling the console.

"We need... to stop?" He spoke in broken English, his eyebrow scrunched up at me.

I shook my head no.

\*

*Let's go back again…* my then-fiancé sent me the
ultimate text message to prompt my moving out. This
was a few weeks after he'd confessed he'd been
unfaithful:

**HIM #3:** BABE. I NEED THE RING BACK.

**ME:** WAIT. WHAT? YOU CHEATED ON ME
WITH SOME CELEBRITY COOK AND—WAIT.
LEMME GET THIS STRAIGHT. YOU WANT ME
TO GIVE YOU BACK THE RING YOU PROPOSED
TO ME WITH?

**HIM #3:** SHE'S PREGNANT. THAT RING WAS REALLY EXPENSIVE.

**ME:** I'M SO CONFUSED AS TO HOW THIS IS MY ISSUE?

*

After getting knocked down so many times, my pain taught my mind how to survive. I developed the type of sadness that made parts of my insides die while I fought to stay alive.

This... was how I started making wishes I had to believe in.

I guess I should understand, after all, he'd said; her having a baby *was* financially taxing. He'd asked me to have a child for him a few years prior, but I was too afraid to jump, and my son was still just a young boy. I'd already been jumping through hoops and jumping out of his way as he jumped to conclusions—there was no way I was going to jump into an even deeper deep end and drown even more.

By the time we'd had that conversation, I'd already pawned the ring and bought a $10,000 camera with the money. The camera never took any good pictures.

\*

I soon developed the type of madness that made me just a little more willing to believe in anything. Even if it weren't anything I could see or touch. Cue imaginary world, people, and in it—everything safe. Any love I'd ever seen or touched crumbled, but ever since I was a tiny girl, my imagination was always a better world than this one.

A place that couldn't possibly fall down, at least not in my head.

So what if it was all just make-believe? Pretending was far better than having no hope at all. When I think back on it, I probably built up a dream world by wishing on things I shouldn't ever believe in because that false sense of hope was better than knowing everyone I'd ever believed in had left me hopeless.

When I moved out, Him #3 went missing for two days. And when I say missing, I mean he wasn't answering any of my calls or texts. The part I wasn't ready for was *myself*. Without knowing yourself, you'll be surprised by your own actions. And I was. I was calling his phone like some fiend. I *left him* and thought I'd be fine. I wasn't fine.

We'd been together for about six or seven years—give or take the last one. I thought maybe we'd just talk it over and live in separate places for a while. Perhaps I'm not sure what I thought then. Maybe I hadn't actually planned it all out at all. We were going to talk about it, and we weren't going to argue, and he wasn't going to throw me into any walls this time. But all of that happened, and instead, he just rammed his "I'm sorry" inside me so hard I saw colorful spots. My eyes rolled back. Tears slid down the side of my cheeks, wetting up the pillow.

I took him back, except this time I was paying all the bills in a much smaller apartment, and I'd wanted him so much I'd accepted not being the only one.

Now, *that* was a different type of hurt.

One day, while my son took a nap, I sat in a warm bath. I cried so hard I fell asleep. If he hadn't started whimpering, then crying… I would have drowned.

# CHAPTER 5

# MONEY

I couldn't make this up if I tried. Chase Wealth Management has called again. Gotta love this guy's piss-erverance. You see, I could commit to their minimums, but my fear was, the way life was hitting me, I'd have to pull out everything in zero to three weeks because of some magical life mishap the second I signed up for it. I needed someone to help me manage my finances. I walked into a location near my house and matched the nameplate on the desk to the person I'd spoken with.

# MONEY

**ME:** I THINK I SPOKE WITH YOU OVER
THE PHONE ABOUT SIGNING UP AND MOVING
MY ASSETS TO YOUR ACCOUNTS. SEEMS LIKE
IT'S GONNA BE QUITE THE STRUGGLE, SO I
JUST WANT TO FIND OUT MORE ABO—

**MAN BEHIND THE BIG DESK:** YES, YOU
SPOKE TO ME. I AGREE THAT COULD BE
"QUITE THE STRUGGLE," AS YOU'VE SAID.
BUT WE ASSURE YOU TOP-NOTCH SERVICE
THROUGHOUT THE PROCESS.

**ME:** WAIT. WHAT?

**MAN BEHIND THE BIG DESK WITH THE
NICE WATCH:** WE WILL HAVE 24-HOUR
SUPPORT LINES FOR YOU AS WELL AS A

DESIGNATED ONE-ON-ONE PRIVATE CLIENT BANKER.

*ME:* SO I AM TO GIVE YOU MY LIFE SAVINGS—IN EXCHANGE FOR A PERSON WHO WILL PAY ATTENTION TO ME IN MOMENTS OF CRISIS?

*MAN BEHIND THE BIG DESK WITH THE NICE WATCH, TWIDDLING HIS THUMBS:* [HE'D ALREADY TOLD ME HE TOOK CARE OF HIS WIFE IN OUR INITIAL PHONE INTERVIEW. SHE WAS THERE FOR HIM THROUGH AND THROUGH. SHE WAS ALSO, AN INSTAGRAM MODEL. HE CLEARED HIS THROAT.] SHALL WE?

\*\*\*

Liam went on to marry the mother of his child. By the time I found out, it didn't hurt as much because I'd met Him #4, Dylan.

Him #4 sprang forth full of charm with a hint of arrogance in public, but kitten-saving romantic by nightfall. His mother was a fair-skinned black dermatologist to many celebrities, and his father was a pediatrician. He had the white-guy-next-door-in-jean-shorts-and-flip-flops look for sure. Dylan and his dad were both handsome and had matching dimples. Dylan wore his hair in what was known then as a "curly-top"

and had bright green eyes that sometimes turned hazel.

The butterflies never went away with Dylan. Never.

*

Flash-forward: I STAYED FOR MONEY. THERE, I

SAID IT! But I saw much more than his money, and I'd

always believed everyone should be out for the

"betterment of their own economy." I also worked hard,

wished for a comfortable life, and loved him beyond any

reasonable reason. There was no woman who wouldn't

have wanted him. And yet, he wanted me: In my glasses

squinting at my laptop. No makeup. My hair all over the place. Coffee stains everywhere trying to overexplain everything. He'd just look at me in awe.

"You are the most intelligent woman I have ever met," Dylan said to me inside of a kiss he gave me one rainy day. I was rushing off to take one of the last tests I'd take to complete my undergraduate program.

I finished my degree and would push further. So I was a goal digger as well. I fought hard to find something to be proud of and take pride in.

*

The day Dylan and I met, I was getting a fucking ticket. I was leaving the eye doctor on Main Street in Culver City when I noticed an officer parked across the street behind my car. I froze, too far away to get his attention. I could see him checking out his surroundings. I ran to the crosswalk, pressed the button, and rocked anxiously on my toes, waiting for the light to change. I saw a young man wearing beige khakis and a white collared shirt walking up. He started a conversation with the officer. I watched as the officer's body language changed, and he began to chuckle in the distance. The stranger continued to engage with him, and I saw him point at my car, reach into his pocket, open his hand, sift

through change, and fill my meter. I hit the corner full

speed in my heels and yellow sundress. I was waving my

hands at the stranger and the officer, but not calling out to

avoid causing even more of a scene. A few seconds

before I reached my car, I saw the officer give a cool

salute to the stranger and walk away. As I rushed up to

him, he smiled, both hands in his pockets. He looked

down, then back up at me. He shined those gorgeous

greens and dimples.

"I'm sorry, you're…?"

"Lalanii, thank you, thank you so much! I can give

you, like, a dollar for the quarters .I was just coming out

of the optometrist, and I told the receptionist my meter

was running out, and she just kept going and going…"

"Really, it's no problem. Really. I'm Dylan." He

extended his hand to me and flashed another magazine

smile at me. I couldn't really tell if he was flirting or if he

was just unsure of what to say next. He managed humble

and confident so effortlessly it was astonishing.

"I owe you! I owe you so big. I mean, I totally don't

need another ticket on this car, I have so many. There's

just so much to remember—"

"I was just getting coffee," he said, spotting me

looking in the direction of the café. "If you want, we can

walk a bit and grab a cup. You've got about an hour on

the meter now." His smirk and flirty eyes were at me again.

I reached my right hand over to my left and pinched my wrist quickly, a thing I do when I need to know if something was really happening. "Yes, I owe you a coffee for saving me from a seventy-dollar ticket!"

We walked a few easy steps to cross the street toward the café. His skin was glowing bright and smooth. I flashed him a this-must-be-my-lucky-day smile.

He nodded over at the empty seats and sat.

"Milk or no?" I asked him.

"Black, a little cream, no sugar." His eyes traced my figure, and he blinked slow.

I walked toward the counter with a little bounce in my step.

"You seem real, uh, well put together," he said to me as I sat down with our coffees. I think that must have been his way of saying I looked nice.

Complete opposite, I thought to myself. But, from the outside looking in, I supposed that could be said. My heels were adorned with sunflowers, my sundress had poodle flair, and I had several matching flowers in my hair. I was also taking care of my optometrist appointment months early just so I could pick out new frames. To him, I could seem well put together.

"You must have been popular with the ladies!" I blurted out. I didn't know why I said that—my nervousness maybe? I was a terrible flirt—always have been. I seemed to manage to say something offensive by accident.

"Nah, nah, not at all. That was back in my college days." He didn't take it that way.

"Where'd you go?"

"Well, I was accepted into Loyola, but I just kind of fell off." He sipped.

"You didn't finish?"

First strike. Here we go.

"Well, my mom and dad wanted to move some of their locations to New York, so you know."

"So… what do you do?" I twiddled with my hair and tried to act like I didn't hope he did something he was passionate about and made him lots of money. People who live their purpose were happiest.

"I run my family's business. They have a few offices."

"Ah, I see."

So he seems brilliant but couldn't get along without Mom and Dad. Couldn't finish school. Cute, likely a womanizer, and probably couldn't pass a test if I told him the answers beforehand. I couldn't help but judge—I liked him. I figured asking another question right then would make our coffee chat seem like an interview.

I was batting my lashes slowly and leaving moments of silence. I couldn't help but be excited; this was my first "accidental" date in almost three months. My second semester of school was taking up all of my time.

"All right then, Dylan, it was great to meet you. Thanks for your quick assistance with that umm—"

"Nah, really, it was nothing. And hey, here's my card, if you ever need a dermatologist or anything, my mom— she's great."

"Ok, sure, your mom—?" I repeated. But then I thought to clarify. "So… this is your mom's card?" My face must've shown disapproval. As I looked down, I saw it said his name on the card, so I regretted saying anything.

"No, it's my card, it's my number, but you know she knows more about the lotions and creams and stuff."

"Ohhhhhhh, right." I looked down. I slowed my walk, and I could feel a pop of sweat slide down my back. I flashed him my hope-I -see-you-again smile. He gave me

a hanging wave in the sky and walked back to his white
Range Rover.

*

We started dating from that moment forward. I'd sent
a message to his phone, and he always called me instead
of texting back. Small talk and giggles. We moved in
together within three months, but we were never home.
We chased experiences—every week. Restaurants,
ATVs, Jet Skis, road trips, hikes. It was like we'd been
best friends in another life and had just reunited. I wanted
to be with him any second he could spend with me. I was
Superwoman as a mother and Wonder Woman as a

student. He spoke little motivations into everything I took on.

It was the simple things. The way he smiled into his laughter. He would tickle me in the hallway. Sometimes, when I'd make a decision without him, I could hear his approval or the questions he'd ask me to make sure I was making the right decision. It was like he'd gotten inside of my mind. He would pin me up against the wall to kiss my forehead, then nose, then lips like we were in a movie. Then let me go like it didn't happen. Walk away, then come back and scoop me up into his arms. My legs kicked in the air. If I resisted him in any way, he would give me more attention. What I loved most was his interest in what I was interested in… even though I knew that he knew nothing about it.

    Around him, I always felt more than wanted; there wasn't hesitation, and there was never any doubt. He didn't try to pretend he didn't want me. He had a smoothness about him that just understood—timing. He'd ask my opinion about some of his decisions and ask permission out of respect and consideration—not because he thought I would mind if he used the last of the milk. He'd know when a hug might be necessary or when a nod in acknowledgement or a quick smile was ok. He'd always call me twice because he said my phone was "at the bottom of your purse." Last ring of the second call, I'd pick up.

"Found it," I chuckled, more than once.

When I was with him, I was full. My confidence was so high. I lit up. I loved everyone more because I felt admired. I walked differently. He was my cotton candy sugar rush, and it was like he made it his job to watch my mood and give me a fix the very second I was coming down. He was every opposite of Liam, and let's just say… it was the first time I'd ever felt anyone make me happier.

## Play

just play in my hair and fulfill all my dreams

he unbraided my bad days

said "let me give you some air"

then he kissed me like a winding staircase

and I don't know how I forgot from there

but where are we?

Where?

The day I decided I wanted to marry Him #4, he'd run
me a bubble bath after I'd received two rejection letters

from top-choice magazines for my writing and a matching rejection letter from my top-choice school. Stung like hell. He read the letters and then placed them under a magazine and didn't say a word. He kissed my forehead as one of my straps fell down, then the other. As my top fell to the floor, he undid the drawstring of my high-waist pants and slid my white lace string down. I shivered and thought, *Well great, he believes he can fuck this out of me. Just great.* He scooped me up in a hug and plopped me in warm, sudsy water. Just then, I wished we were going to have wild sex, as I was more terrified of him seeing me cry than anything. It wasn't the rejections; it was the fear of everything not ever getting better, of my wishes and dreams just being wishes and dreams. He leaned over the side of the tub with a beige sponge and

his quiet. I'd always held issues with quiet. I was never

ok with quiet. He begged quiet; he was quiet. The water

rinsed off my back, and I cupped my head in my hands

and cried softly. He said nothing, but he knew what I was

thinking. He picked up the sponge filled with hot-warm

suds and squeezed it over my neck. He poured lavender-

hyacinth oil in the tub. I watched as he walked to the door

to cut the floor steam on and the whole bathroom filled

with hot air. The steam rose. He sat on the side of the tub,

shirtless. He steamed with me until I stopped crying.


Minutes later, when the water was so hot I was weak,

he grabbed a towel and picked me up out of the tub—

wrapped me like a child, holding me as tight as he could for a few more seconds than he needed to. He carried me to our bed and then grabbed his oversized white robe and replaced the towel with it. He slipped me under the covers on his side of the bed and kneeled next to me. I pulled my knees up to my stomach. I felt him pull the damp towel away and out from beneath the robe.

He kissed my forehead. I must have dozed off after he closed the bedroom door.

The next thing I remember was waking up, and it was as though it hadn't happened. Morning. Orange juice to my left. Egg whites and spinach to my right. Coffee in the maker, made. *Poets & Writers* magazine was on the table next to me, opened to a page. He'd circled a few opportunities. He didn't say anything about the night before. He never mentioned it at all.

We lived together in a lovely condo in Hermosa Beach. It had walk-in his-and-her closets and a beautiful open kitchen. At first, it took me a minute to understand how it all happened, and it was hard that my broke starving artist/collegiate wannabee but-gotta-buy-used-books-life was in the big leagues, but, just like everything else, it became second nature.

Some things are innately in my heart, however. My mother's we-don't-waste-no-damn-food-in-this-house thinking, and getting the last out of any container: shampoo, soap, toothpaste, anything. It drove Dylan crazy. Apparently, rich people just waste a lot of toothpaste and don't have time to roll it up or add water to any solution to get the last of it.

I did ok living in downtown Culver City, but this had nothing on a born into old money business mogul and a doctor who went boating lifestyle. No, Dylan's parents were, in two lovely words, lucrative and loaded.

\*

The love was so hard it was like choking on a chicken bone. The wishing one. Fuck you gon' do when you're already choking but grab at your neck and hope someone saves you?

His mom had a ratchet way of showing off her success. Such shenanigans settled in nicely at her vacation home, conveniently our first Thanksgiving together. Their relationship seemed perfect. If Bill Cosby's character on *The Cosby Show* had been a white guy, he most definitely would've been Dylan's dad.

Dylan wore pocketed linen pants and a matching newsboy cap. He walked away with his hands in his pockets, leaving me with a wink as if now was my big

chance to get to know his mother. A few moments later, I

heard him in the distance, making jokes with his dad.

His mom, however, was at the other side of my table,

not whispering at all—staring with dead, cold eyes.

"Are you on birth control?" she said to me.

I hesitated, shifted, and looked in Dylan's direction. I

wanted to tell this stupid broad how nasty her son was,

about how we fucked wildly on a regular—the covers

never stay on the bed—that sometimes the feathers fly

out the pillows and he sucks tits like he's making a new

kingdom… come to think of it, I was just sucking his—

"Bae, you ok?" Dylan interrupted as he walked up to the table.

I must have zoned out after his mom's question. I couldn't believe that *that* was the conversation she wanted to have, especially the first time I'd met her. But this was what rich people worried about… their children impregnating what they believed to be the wrong women. The maid came around to offer a Danish and tuna appetizer; I took the Cabernet.

## Invest In Me

Invest in me

Buy me pale pink vases full of Paper Mates and erasures

And dresser drawers of trinkets and Tide commercial

colored wash towels

I'll pay you back with amazingness

Invest in me

I'll give you a shy restless anxiousness, but I'll dress up

like your waitress

Invest in me

I'll make the bedspread make up itself

I'll make my fingertips skip up your left side

I'll make your cheeks blush with very few words or

warning,

Invest in me

Buy me knee socks, buy me houses, buy me bookstores

with three sections of poetry and bay windows. Buy me

suggestions that talk shit to each other buy me that

makeshift bakery starter kit so I can not bake you

anything and tell everyone I did.

Invest in me

I'll be good

…

Buy me albino gummy bears from gosh knows where.

And buy me a light blue pitchfork to dig up everything

that hurt and then bury it deeper

Invest in me

I'll love you with nothing else in the way

Get me pink pancakes with blackberry blueberries

Get me lightning on the page

…

Invest in me

Buy me a television I can put my own words in

Make me a latté that stirs in my bloodstream

Pick me up one of those everlasting beds of pillows

The kind that resembles spaceships with windows

Buy me a mirror that tells me I'm beautiful even when

I'm not looking at him

Buy me a snowball that's not cold

A snow cone not too sweet

A snow mountain I can balance on long enough to scream

down without crying like a three-year-old

Invest in me, invest in me

I will not call you fiction


Invest in me

                                With no variation

Buy me white carnations and use your imagination when

you name them

    Baby can you get my dreams down,

          I can't reach,

               I can't reach.

# WINGS

As soon as we weren't together, he became harder to reach. I would get voicemail three times before he could answer a call.

SOMETIMES IT'S NOT LOVE.

YOU JUST GET STUCK IN A HICCUP.

**hic·cup**

/ˈhikəp/

*An involuntary spasm of the diaphragm and respiratory*

*organs that can happen as a force of nature, or a reaction*

*to—laughter, fear, or love.*

He got *different.*

It's harder to keep up a visage over time, and there are parts of a person (when keeping a secret life) that just want to be found out. Maybe it began when Dylan started law school, you know—people change when they go into rigorous programs. I'm not sure, but I'm incredibly sure of the night everything changed for me. I remember it like it happened only a few moments ago.

*It was my birthday, and it was a night I would never forget—one I also wish I could never remember.*

*

They were the same peach roses I'd seen atop the
toilet in our bathroom at home. Him #4's cleaning lady
had them special ordered, I thought. One had fallen
behind the toilet, and the tip was covered in blood. When
I saw our stunning peach roses in our bathroom the next
morning, I remembered a little.


I was staring at his diamond cufflinks as I woke—a
bundle of peach roses strewn across our light grey
comforter, as if to say, I'm sorry. I had a headache. I tried
to think back as far as I could.

.

He'd said ok. Eight to midnight, he'd said ok. I'd said ok, but I had another thing in mind, and but it was fine enough for me for now, it was alllll fine. The birthday celebrations would start soon enough, and I was over the moon and stars with delight. My dress had been professionally tailored in the most delightful hi-low flow, backless, fitted to flare. The makeup girl was twenty minutes early; she'd wanted to discuss colors early on, but there had been no time. The jewelry team arrived to go over the specifics while we sipped champagne on our balcony. I had never worn $300,000 worth of jewelry, but Dylan assured me, "Baby this is your night, and I love you," and I said ok, and we'd signed the paperwork for it because it was borrowed like his models, he said the jewelry was borrowed like for his high-end models, and I thought nothing of it because you know I could almost be a model except maybe I wore oversized glasses and didn't have the confidence but, "Yes, babe, you can model," he said. The look on his face was magic stolen from the sky.

*

So I'd had on all of these jewels and was decked in moonlight and kisses from him. I told him I wanted to be a model now. He squinted his eyes back at me. It took all of my concentration just to put on both heels at the same time—I stumbled a bit. He flashed a smile at me.

Dylan had specific instructions about how the night was going to go, but I wasn't having it. Just because it was technically a model party he was working didn't mean it wasn't still my birthday, and any birthday in my twenties had two things in common: laughter and belligerence. For instance, he'd discussed with me several times, explaining the reasons I would need a security detail at all times, and I could not bring any of my friends. Well, hell, what the heck—I didn't have very many anyway. We were picked up in a limo. He'd been whispering sweet whatevers to me.

So yeah, the limo arrived, and he helped me in and cozied up next to me. He was fidgety, but my God, I was a sucker for a man in a white tux. My shimmering semi-see-through dress matched. We were poised for any magazine. His green eyes sang me "Happy Birthday," crawling his fingertips upside my thigh line as he mouthed the words. Then he held my face in his hands the way he would after we made love. I'd slept only about four hours; I'd been so excited. I couldn't eat a thing all day. It wasn't the cost of the dress, or the sparkling shoes, the jewelry, or the makeup… it was the enchantment of it all. I remember feeling seen. It wasn't the spoils that made it that way; it was his attention and the energy he put into it all.

The second we arrived, I had to go pee. Such bad timing.

As we walked in, Dylan's hand guided me slowly and patiently into his world. The air was thick and cold. My neck was heavy with the jewels.

"Baby, it's ok, but you'll need a security guard to go with you. Is it ok if I have my friend Niam… Niam can go with you. I have to greet a few people, then I'll be back for your birthday dance…" His voice trailed off.

One second I felt like I was the only one in the orbit of all planets, the next second he was gone.

Sparkling gems flooded the necks and earlobes of all of the women. A few crowds passed fast, several floated by, most nearly knocking me over. I could hear my thoughts, and they were screaming, Yes, *I want this life, yes!* If my heels made too loud of a noise, people would turn to stare; I had to glide. I picked up quickly.

He used to tell me he was stuck in a world, but it wasn't of this world. This was after I'd charged at him about what he did for a living and showed up twice to a dermatology office he didn't actually work in.

"I host parties for models sometimes. I help my mom out at her office too." His lie swayed.

It wasn't until this second of wandering the foyer of a banquet hall alone—security detail in sight, but distracted—that I understood why I hadn't been invited before. He was perfectly gone.

We never got that dance, and I didn't make it to the bathroom right then. I'd been told by security that there were several bathrooms, but the ones upstairs were the ones "the women used." I caught eyes with him briefly on the way down the hallway toward the stairs, but he was surrounded by an audience of fishtails or flowy dresses and suits. When I saw that, I went to the second room I saw, and I began to chat with a well-dressed gentleman. The one security guard trailed not too far from me—still.

The man I saw had a grey textured mustache and reminded me of a white Obama. He was dapper, right out of a *GQ* magazine. He made no advances; he just glared at my neck like he'd been a vampire in his previous life. Maybe I'd watched too many movies.

And then he said the strangest thing.

"So, Miss, what land is yours?"

"Excuse me?"

And I was supposed to know how to answer this question. But since I didn't, I was gonna wing it like I did. Replying as though I didn't hear him initially gave me a few seconds to think up a better reply.

"I own everything. I belong everywhere, I run the landfill, and I recycle." I said this all with a wry smile, tossing my hair back. Comfortable, like it was nothing.

"Aha, well then, I'll speak to my associate at the top of the hour. I'll show you what I own."

I felt like I didn't know enough to keep up witty banter or coy conversation, so my only option was to stay as intriguing as possible and have the last confident word— then walk away slowly. So I walked away.

I didn't see that guy again right away. It was like he disappeared, like Dylan had begun to do so often. His intrigue lay on me, so familiar. He was distinguished and poised, and he seemed to sit atop my shoulder. He was

the type of person you couldn't ask a question he
wouldn't have the answer to, a person who already knew
what your best interests were, who studied you and your
mannerisms because he didn't lose direct eye contact
even once. The behavior was so much like Dylan,
*familiar*. It was like he'd been "trained" for me.

I mingled.

I wandered more. I walked long enough to forget I'd
been searching for the bathroom as the urge had subsided.
It was the most beautiful place I'd ever seen. Two women
stood off to the side of the main room, sipping red
wine… I felt like I could blend in as long as I didn't talk

too much or too fast. I could hardly stop my thoughts.
Maybe thirty minutes to an hour had gone by.

I felt a light wind coming from a massive centerpiece
waterfall of wine. Must have cost a fortune. It was
beautiful. Above the fountain was a shimmering
chandelier. I picked up my glass, held it under the spout,
and wine poured right in. I started a conversation with the
sparkling women nearby. They were dazzled in jewels
like mine and had longer-than-shoulder-length hair, and
their eyelashes seemed to be in 3D.

Naomi looked the oldest, at least twenty-one, but Cai.
Cai carefully pronounced and spelled her name, was
outgoing, and forced her smile too much; she seemed to

not be of drinking age at all, perhaps? Naomi was quieter but leaned in when she spoke, and her eyes responded to every word. I'd asked them both what they did, and somehow neither of them had responded, but the conversation continued. I asked them about the guy in the grey suit who'd intrigued me, but they hadn't seen him. Another young girl who looked not yet twenty floated over, and we chatted about the jewels around my neck. The more compliments I received, the more I wished I had my friends, at least some of them, to celebrate my birthday with me.

Dylan grabbed at my arm playfully to pull me closer to him. I felt the ladies stare with jealousy. He could have been, after all, a model in his own right. He had the kind of stature women have dreams of. I know, as I've had some. He whispered to me.

"And you, you in this dress. I cannot wait to put you to bed…"

"Dylan, this is the best birthday ever; you know I can't dance!" I said as he twirled me and then slowed to a stop.

"To many more, you're worth it."

He had one arm around my waist, but my mind drifted off to Mr. GQ. I had no idea why.

"I met this guy just now, Mr. GQ, and some girls over at the wine fountain."

"Mr. who?" Obviously, that wasn't his name; I realized I didn't get his name.

"He looked like a white Obama."

"Oh, you mean Andy, yeah, stay away from him. He's no good. Not a good guy at all. Unless you mean Derrick, and he isn't good either, come to think of it. Are you ready, babe? I'm going to wrap up here in a few."

"One more drink, one more," I told him, flinging my head back. I wanted to meet more people and see more things. *I'm going over to this wine waterfall, and I'm going to sip a tad more. He should let me enjoy myself,* I thought.

I guzzled four of those mini chandelier glasses of wine. It was time for some action. About fifteen minutes later, I was racing to find a bathroom, because my urge to pee had come back with a vengeance. My "double security detail" seemed to have diminished to one, and he was distracted by one of the sparkling girls. The entire downstairs had no bathroom! I was lost. I was in this environment of weirdos and fancy folks, and I couldn't find anywhere to pee. I wobbled around, barely able to move since the slit in my skirt prevented it. I began to ask around, but everyone either shrugged or acknowledged me with silent indifference.

I wandered. It had to be approaching 11:30 or so by now. After this, I would look for Dylan. Enough fun for little ol' me, I guess. Being lost had started to get annoying.

Up the swiveling staircase I went. I wandered down the hallway. The view alone was magnificent, all white with peach roses in the vases at every table beneath each awning like what I wanted on our wedding day.

"You."

"You." Mr. GQ said back. "Not sure where you ran off to." He peered to the left, looking off to the distance where I could only see what looked like closed bedroom doors.

"Well, I just need to use the little girl's room now. Then I'm off."

"Oh well, you can't leave just yet."

"And why is that?" I said. His eyebrow rose as he scratched his head. I noticed one of his cuffs was undone. He had diamond cufflinks.

"Well, I haven't gotten you a drink or told you my name."

"Well, if we cross paths again…" I snapped back at him, quickly remembering that the thing I needed to do, right away, was pee.

"If you'd like a drink, I'll be downstairs," he said.

"Thanks," I said, smirking and turning in the other direction, as I walked away.

Inside the rooms, each bathroom was locked. Every door. I swear it, I was going to pee myself in my pretty dress and diamonds. This would be an exact tragedy. I ran to the second door. Locked again. I heard noises behind it, so I knocked louder. No one opened.

No one opened the next one, and no one opened the next one.

Desperate now as the wine had taken over, I push-held the next door, assuming it was locked. I rammed my side, attempting to break the lock entirely.

"Ohhhffff!"

There was a puddle and stains of blood everywhere around the toilet in the bathroom. A small girl with an oval face and dark brown hair (who didn't look older than fourteen) was crying bold tears down her face, and she was crouching. I immediately forgot about my needs. I bent down as my heart pounded.

"Are you ok! What can I do? Are you hurt?"

The girl heaved and held herself between her legs. I crouched lower and immediately thought about Mr. GQ's grey suit and his cufflinks, his diamond cufflinks. The cufflink I'd noticed was undone when I last saw him. One was missing.

"What can I do!"

I was now making more noise than I was sure she'd intended, as she seemed to be hiding quietly. The girl was now in full panic; I'd made matters worse. She was crouched lower down and sobbing loudly now. She had been responding, but it just wasn't in any language I could understand. I didn't know what she'd been saying. She was bleeding heavily. She was getting worse, her heaving had become a holler, and I couldn't help her, I couldn't help her if I stood here, but I'd gone into some sort of shock.

I stood with her as I tried to grab her, but she kept hunching lower to the ground as though moving was not of preference.

I decided to try and pick her up, but she was heavier than I imagined. I squatted down beside her, forgetting I was in a dress. I screamed, hoping the half-open door would allow someone to hear. We sat there for what seemed like an hour. A peach rose was sitting next to her, the tips were covered in blood, and the floor was streaked the same. I was stuck between leaving a child bleeding between her legs alone or going for help. I could see she was wounded, and blood was brightening and darkening at the same time in patches of her clothes. She started to cry less. She was losing too much blood. I grabbed white hand towels and placed them over her private area where I could see, and I turned her from sitting on the floor next to me to lying propped up against the wall and the toilet. I ran to the top of the stairs, and I screamed his name.

"Dylannnnnn!" I heard a commotion from the party in the distance.

Dylan showed up at the bottom of the stairs, alarmed. My arms and fingers were covered in streaks of blood. He ran up to me and grabbed me like precious property. I didn't have to say anything before he was forcing me down the stairs, running much faster than I could... I was struggling with my footing and trying to speak. I saw a rush of people going up the stairs in quick steps.

"We have to go, babe. We have to go now." He looked at me, eyebrows scrunched with both fear and anger.

"There's a girl, she's bleeding badly, she's been bleeding, I called for you, I've been screaming for you, this—" My voice trailed off as my nose snot ran into my mouth. Tears ran down my neck.

Somehow I ended up in the limo; there was our driver and far-off voices. The driver offered me soda water; I finished in two gulps. Next, I heard paramedics, but I couldn't recall anyone calling. I was passing out as though I'd been drugged heavily. I felt wetness and could see I'd peed on myself, but my body was stalled. I could not react. My eyes were tired, and my arms were heavy. I fought to stay awake and heard him whisper as I faded.

"I shouldn't have brought you here. Everything will be fine, you won't even remember. Love you, babe."

. . .

The last thing I could recall was Dylan sliding the diamond necklace off my neck, covered in almost-dried blood. He then slipped off the one shiny heel I still had left on. I was somehow in our bed. I passed out staring into his diamond cufflinks. They looked exactly like Mr. GQ's. Dylan was sort of dapper too. Like out of a magazine, really.

*

Because I used to tease him and say he wasn't gon' be shit but a spender of his parents' money, he went and got his damn law degree. He chose commercial law because a criminal lawyer would have just given him away, I think. His photographic memory and knack for talking girls clean outta their good sense proved to be enough to make him a healthy waste of my time, but clearly he had the whole package: looks, intellect, money—the perfect gentleman. Well, except he and his delightful crew sold children to high-end celebrities and rich people on every third weekend. Allegedly.

I'd apparently never heard of love from afar, so after I started to piece it together, I couldn't do anything. I had no definitive proof, so I kept right on giddying up into his labyrinth.

Surprisingly, I wasn't even upset at my decision when the walls started to blur, and I couldn't get out, I was just there. I hadn't realized how much I wanted a baby girl and how ironic that would turn out to be. And then it hit me. Having the child of the head lawyer of a fake consulting cover business or a rep at his mom's doctor's office, having a child for a man who might have co-

conspired to run the largest upscale private "modeling" business ever to shift from Los Angeles to New York would probably not be the most excellent idea.

The next week started to look like the next week and then the next week. There was shopping, and there were high-end bars—always. There were travel plans, but they started to get pushed a week apart, then one and a half then finally two weeks apart. He loved to buy shoes to make up for lost time. Shoes didn't talk or keep you company no matter how expensive they were, and trust me, when I was wearing something so expensive, I didn't wanna be seen by anyone except for the one who bought me the damn heels as if to say to him,

"See, look what you did? Look at how much more beautiful I am!" As if to think, *I wasn't pretty enough to myself until he saw me or I was only pretty if he said so.*

If a stranger were to wink, I felt guilty, even. It was like being owned. Him #4 never had to ask me for not one favor. I would've done anything. Another few months of this, and I was bored, scared, and lonely.

YOU DON'T NEED MONEY

IF YOU DON'T HAVE TIME.

YOU DON'T NEED TIME

IF YOU DON'T HAVE HEALTH.

The most important thing to me was time: I was going out of my mind with sadness, worry, and wonder. It was a different type of "sentenced to silence" fear. Dylan never asked me to keep any secrets. I just loved him, so I asked minimal questions, and when I was confused, I stood very still to listen intently for the truth. I was aware, but I did not let him know how much I thought I knew.

\*

And then I blew up. It got real.

Him #4 aka Mind-Fuck, aka Mr. It's Everyone Else's Fault, aka Dylan thought omission was not a form of lying. For over three years, I dated this man who, upon introduction, told me he worked at his mother's office—without ever telling me what he actually did for a living. At the point of undeniable question, when I simply could not stand not being sure if I knew what he really did, he very plainly said to me,

"I am not a liar just because you haven't been paying attention."

I inhaled sadly.

Through this time, I'd helped his photographic memory pass the bar the first time around. Instead of watching him open his own law office, I watched him return to his hidden industry. When I had to visit my morals, perhaps him selling drugs might have been better, but I just wanted better. I just wanted a better person. If I had known more of his business or actually been included, I might have gone to jail as an accomplice… possibly, if what he *could've been* into, he'd *actually been* into. But I didn't know for sure. None of this seemed to bother him, and he wasn't interested in explaining.

All I could think about was how he played the role of wanting to be a lawyer so well.

All I could think about was the family I was not going to have now.

## He Said to Write through It

*We make the mistake of thinking the people we love will understand us enough, we make the mistake of believing in that trust, we make the mistake of sharing too much. I would never again be this quiet, because then, how will anyone else know what I needed?*

he said to write through it.

nausea. the nauseous nausea the warp the shortness of breath the different

colors of the alphabet the grown-upness. the kisses on the cheek, the best friend i lost in the process the helpless.

the way his eyes lit up my world over linguini. the way he held my hand. all the way through the landing. and then.

he said to write on the mirror upside down on the ceiling he said to write on my inner elbow he said to write while i'm dreaming and wake up and recite what i've seen.

he said to love him, i said I can't. he said to love him, i said i did.

he said i got nervous i said, i'll be damned.

and wouldn't you know. it was perpetual it was regrettable it was un-everything i could ever be, i am so against who i have come to be. he said write through it, i said i'm freezing.

flushing it all out. pale yellow. he's heavy, it's all blurry.

it's all up against what it is…

he said to write through it.

i thought i did.

# WINGS

...WHEN DO MY WINGS GROW IN? WHEN?

# CHAPTER 6

## SHIT

Frantic shuffling from another part of the house. It had to be a little after six in the morning. Dylan had already left for the airport the night before without any luggage. Someone was in our house. Before I could reach the hallway, a man grabbed and squeezed my neck. His face was unmasked. He wore all black with oversized swamp boots. I felt the urgency in his movements; he did not mean to just scare me. People who intended to keep you alive did not reveal their faces.

"Where are the papers?" He spoke in a low voice.

I whimpered, unable to speak. My eyes grew big, and I could stare only in the direction the man pointed my head. I couldn't see another person, but there was shuffling in the next room.

The stranger called a number, and I heard my Dylan's voice answer in his usual busy hello.

"Where are the papers? Are you trying to fuck us? Because if you're trying to fuck us, I have your pretty bitch here, and she's just dying to get fucked." The man chuckled like he'd been waiting to say that.

I struggled to scream something, hoping I'd be heard, but I couldn't. My elbow knocked my planter into the sink—baby basil and dirt everywhere. He let go of my throat so I could speak. Happening like a dream awake, scared breathing inside of scared thinking, I was in so much shock I wasn't even there.

The phone line went blank; he was gone before I could tell him I loved him. A coffee sat on the table with a colorful coffee sleeve. I heaved in my chest.

*

We'd lived in Hermosa Beach for a little over six months. I remember specifically moving there because of this coffee shop. My favorite coffee shop; I went there at least three times a week. Java Man.

"Ohhhh babe, look at how cute this little place is, baby, it's all colorful with the tables, couches, and chairs!" Dylan wasn't listening, he was on his phone, but he looked up and smiled.

We weren't too far, this little 1920s-styled bungalow. Local art displayed on the walls and the middle-aged men behind the counter all playfully flirted with my indecisiveness every time I came in. One time he mocked me.

"Not a latte this morning, Miss?"

"Yes, no, yeah, but can you add a shot, never mind, just make it, nevermin', but make that two."

"Two coffee mm' espresso, yes, no, yes, haha!" the man behind the counter repeated.

A minute or so later, he handed me my coffees in colorful sleeves. I tried to taste it, but it was too hot. I burned the tip of my tongue, so I just held it. I remembered thinking, *I should've gotten two coffee sleeve thingies*, but I had already walked outside.

I was staring at the coffee in the colorful coffee sleeves on the table, a tiny bit of steam floating from the top.

\*

I was going to be raped and murdered by two men who went for coffee at my favorite coffee shop before conveniently stopping by my condo. The lone coffee sat on the table as I tried to catch my breath. One man paced my house in killer boots, occasionally moving things but not destroying them. His face was so typical when I looked at him I'd already forgotten his features. I kept trying to replay stuff I would say to the cops once they arrived, if I ended up safe. Things I would say once I was shaking and wearing that blanket worn by survivors after they've been rescued from a tree or a burning house. I kept thinking of things I would remember about my attackers. Tall, pale-skinned males, dark eyes, both dark hair, no accents, wearing all black with white T-shirts showing under their black sweatshirts and matching boots. Great. I'd recalled nothing anyone would be able to point out a person with.

"Tell your bitch ass man he better find me, or I'll be back [here] for the papers."

He slammed me against the side of my pantry door; the force made my head feel numb. It looked like he was going to push me again, so I grabbed the coffee off the table, pulling off the top in one swoop and throwing it at his face. It missed his face and got everything below his shoulders in a full splash. He grabbed me by my neck, squeezing me tighter this time; my eyes bulged, and I was lightheaded in a few seconds, regretting what I'd done.

"C'mon, man, let's go, man, leave the bitch there, she's dead anyway, she's dead." The other man's voice came in, but all I could think was *Oh my God I can't die like this.*

He let my neck go.

The two men rushed out of the back door, and I leaned over until I fell down. I put my head against the cold white floor and let my head shake as I cried. I was getting sleepy as I saw Dylan rushing in.

\*\*\*

The next few weeks weren't possible. Fourteen different medications for seven weeks.

Blackouts were real. Panics and anxieties.

Everything would turn grey in various shades.

I took a handful of antidepressants and calm-down-please pills, some solving problems—but most creating more.

All for different everythings.

When I would wake up, only one eye would open, I'd
be dizzy, my head would hurt, and I'd begin throwing up
in a dark pink tinged with blood. Once, I was gripping the
side of the bed and standing there for hours. It was like
the wind was knocked out of me, but it stayed out of me.
Breathing at all was just scary and hard.

I discovered the medicine took away my creativity. I
couldn't write. I couldn't do anything. Paranoid. I asked
Dylan for time. I wouldn't answer his calls. He wouldn't
stop calling.

I couldn't think about our relationship after my safety
was compromised. I couldn't picture lazy rich trust fund

babies growing up without a mother or a father should

authorities find something amiss. I wanted hard-working

kids. I wanted legacies built by bricks, not break-ins. I

couldn't stomach the thought of him, all debonair while I

was begging a hostile stranger for my life. I couldn't even

form a lot of words when he called to talk. I didn't know

what to say:

**HIM:** HOW ARE YOU?

**ME:** DROWNING IN THAT DAY. IT KEEPS
REPLAYING IN MY MIND. MAKE IT STOP.

**HIM:** SAME.

**ME:** LOOKS LIKE THE SAME DAY, TOO.
THEY ALL LOOK JUST THE SAME.

There were so many conversations we had. Me crying into the receiver. Me sobbing into the top of Dylan's shoulder, begging him to give up everything that was faulty in his life for me. For love.

There was a point in every relationship when I believe both people just understood it wasn't going to get any better.

\*

I had all of my bags already packed into my car when his car pulled up—fast. I imagined he was coming straight from the airport. I bit my lip, and I could see in his eyes he knew there wasn't a thing he could say or do.

He walked over to me slowly, like he held the detonator for a bomb that was about to go off.

"No, no…"

"I am just not interested in being in this—"

"Just come inside, let's talk. I'm off the whole week."

"No, you know what my life is like with you? It's like sugar to shit, really, no one would actually believe it."

I pushed past him and adjusted the edge of my jacket to pat my wet eyes. I got in my car and laid my head on the steering wheel. I looked up, I saw him in the distance. I drove off.

A few months later, I saw my gorgeous Louis Vuitton luggage in the background of our old house on some girl's social media profile. She looked much like the ex he claimed he didn't talk to anymore. He came to my house several times to speak with me through my door.

He'd begged me, and I said he'd have to give up his lifestyle.

"Please don't do this, we're ok, we're not *unhappy*." He'd mocked the way I used to repeat and repeat to him how unhappy *he'd* made me.

I took the screenshot I'd found online of him a few days prior, circled my luggage in the background next to the woman, and texted it to him. I heard him scoff. I imagined him walking back to his car, his face blank, his posture still sure it'd blow over. Seconds later, muted music started, and he drove off.

He'd made it all up, this whole world for me. This person who didn't house women all over the world, promising them modeling contracts, or whatever the promise was, this person who loved me. This person was full of wishes he'd made up from a wish list he'd studied. A wish list that belonged to me. A wish list he'd saved that no longer mattered.

I quit all of the medicine. I enrolled in school again.

My world turned back to color, but my heart and

everything else stayed grey.

Let me go back:

So I actually took Dylan back again, and when I think about it now, I can't believe it either. Yes, I took him back one last time because the pain of how it ended would choke me in my sleep harder than those men in black boots did in my memory. We made love twice. I then followed him to New York for three weeks—only to get sick and have him send me back to LA for the next four. When he finally showed back up five weeks later, I welcomed him too willingly. One night shortly after that, I was jolted awake by a sharp pain.

"You ok?" Dylan asked softly as I grasped the side of the bed.

"It doesn't matter; usually, you're not ever here. I'm fine."

"Come on, Lay, you know I have to work, you know this."

My eyes glazed over—bored of the conversation. I gripped the bed tighter and breathed in slower and felt extremely dizzy. I sat, legs half hanging off the side of the bed.

"I'm tired, I'm just tired."

"Of me?"

"Of you not being the person you were supposed to be for me."

"You moved out, not me. I didn't leave you. You left me." Dylan was flat.

Annoyed, I walked to the kitchen and retrieved a glass to pour some juice into.

"People came into our house and threatened my life!" I yelled at him from the kitchen. "You said you were done, but you lied to appease me, you lie and then tell me nothing, you build up this wall to keep me out—you're supposed to build a wall to keep me safe!"

I was breathing heavier now, words crying out of my mouth like a hot spell. My underarms popped in sweat. I wasn't just going to just sit back and listen to him tell me bits and pieces of lies trying to answer the questions I'd been asking.

"Hey, you're turning all red. Look, let's not get all worked up about this again. I'm sorry, I can't say it any other way. This isn't how things will go. I'm telling you. I need you to trust me, give me time. Why don't you just back in here and go to sleep?"

I went back to the room, without the juice, and closed the door. He trailed behind a few minutes later. I whimpered myself to sleep with my back to him. This would usually be the part when I wanted him to touch me, but we'd been through this so many times before when or if he did so, I'd just say he wasn't going to "fuck away the answers I needed" or "trick me into sex and amnesia again."

The next morning, I woke up dizzy again and drove myself to urgent care. Dylan wasn't home. I skirted into the parking lot nauseated and parked across the handicap space sideways. Must have been something I'd eaten. The first thing the nurse asked me was if I was pregnant.

"Nah, I'd be in here looking like a sad kitten," I said, smirking. I bulged my eyes out sarcastically. "Can you get me something for these dizzy spells?"

A few minutes later, the nurse came back, prefacing what a beautiful kitten I looked like, but I didn't get the joke. "Lalanii, you're pregnant," she clarified.

"What? That's fuckin' imposs—" I responded.

But was it, though? Was it really impossible? I tried to remember. Was it the night weeks ago when Dylan appeared: a lackluster smile in our doorway, as the hallway lights beamed on his linen suit. He simply walked over, grabbed my shoulders from behind the couch softly—yet firmly—and my clothes melted right off.

Or was it another time when he'd tried to ensure my safety with a gift card to self-defense classes, new locks for the house, and, of course, installing a top-notch alarm system. In ways I knew we lacked in chemistry, we made up for in understanding.

One look up from my book, one quick turn of his head from behind the separating wall in our kitchen, and several mundane responsibilities… and he knew, at any of those seconds, much like the moment anyone ever knows to turn on music, or the moment two people make a toast together without permission from one another… it was just that… it was just there. Like the baby in my womb.

This reflection of circumstances… if I had just not gotten so excited if I had only slowed down if I had just taken hold of my emotions…

Dylan was elated when I told him the news. But it felt like my heart immediately transformed into an Etch A Sketch in the weeks that followed: not beating, just shaking. I was jumpy and paranoid, scared, but overall; I just kept replaying his lifestyle and how I thought it would affect our unborn child. We both couldn't stop talking about the baby. We wanted a girl. The very idea of her, of our new reality, masked all the problems I might have had with him. All of them were "maybe" issues now. He "might have" sold children on the black market and called himself a model host or tourist or producer, but he was home every night now, rubbing on my not-yet-existent abdomen with a little pea-sized baby in there—swimming around peacefully, I imagined. I'd throw up toast for thirty minutes, heaving into the toilet bowl, and then I'd slowly and calmly show up at our kitchen table to green tea and crackers. The note next to them read:

"She'll be beautiful, just like you."

We still had our brunch weekly at The Grove and date nights—just with sparkling apple juice. Dylan managed to get dressed each time (and not only in his relaxed suits I loved so much) in a nice pair of jeans that fit him like the top model he could have been, with a white T-shirt, un-tucked, and loafers. His hazel eyes went bright green in the sun's glare. Everything about him was like a postcard very far away.

The next month was bliss. I started to settle in and to accept the life of what "us" was going to feel like. I began to forget some of the pain we'd been through, even though anxiety came back in flashes of panic through my bloodstream any time the phone rang to alert me there was a visitor or a package had arrived. If Dylan was later than 7:01 in the evening, or if I called and he didn't answer on the third ring, I immediately began to worry I'd be raising my child alone.

*

I kept prepping myself for the way I would introduce him to everyone when I finally had to, and these self-talks

were like rehearsing for a play I didn't want to be part of.
No one in my family had met Dylan yet; when I'd go
back and forth from our houses, he'd wait downstairs in
the car. I'd started preparing rebuttals and counters for
uncomfortable questions about the specifics I knew my
sister would ask about the stranger's baby I was having.

"Bae, I have to leave in a few weeks, but I'm going to
leave you a card so you can 'play' with ideas for the
nursery—don't go crazy," he said to me one morning at
our breakfast table. He gave me a smirk-smile, half
dimple showing. He'd already asked me to move back in
with him, and my acceptance was contingent upon him

continuing to *try for us* and keeping up this *good behavior*.

The shutters were always one-third open, and it was usually warm whatever day of the week. My eyes glazed over, not having heard anything beyond *leave in a few weeks*. It was like those words were leading me to accept he was just faking like he was the *perfect boyfriend* or *almost baby daddy*. My heart broke again just in that one sentence.

A week after that breakfast, he slid out of bed at four for a six a.m. flight to New York. I rolled over half asleep and squeezed his arm, and he leaned down and kissed my forehead. He slid the covers back slightly. Both of his warm hands held me below my breast, touching my low abdomen, and he kissed, five long seconds—it seemed— his pinky grazing my raisin areola now perking through my nightie as he raised back up.

I felt him switch on the nightlight in the hallway for me. I heard him set the alarm with his voice, and the door swung to a swift, cushy close.

As soon as he left, my world spiraled. Where was he really going? Was he going to be ok? Would I be safe? What was I gonna do without him?

Earlier that same week, we'd found out she was a girl via private scan. Thirteen-and-a-half-ish weeks—much further along than when I'd decided to have my son as a teenager and ran out of an abortion clinic. In this fourteenth week, she bled down the back of my leg. A thick clot came first, and I screamed myself out of bed, holding my stomach and crunching over, looking at the floor. I saw the thin line of blood, and I fumbled my cell and got his voicemail. I called for an hour nonstop as I drove myself to the hospital in a nightgown, a half-open robe, and my house slippers. All I could think was: *My body would have held her if he hadn't left.*

The nurse came in with a blanket following the doctor's news. She offered me something to drink. She gave me instructions for passing the rest of my child. She set up an appointment for me to return. Dylan was still unreachable.

I told myself she would have been a good girl. Sometimes, I still talk to her when I talk in my sleep, and surely I'm dreaming of her; hence, the dreamcatchers I hung from my bedpost.

I scolded her for not listening to me when I told her to be safe and to stay on her "good behavior." I scolded her for not making it here. I scolded her for not being strong enough.

"I guess you and your dad couldn't really behave much."

"You were supposed to be strong!" I whispered to my empty body.

\*\*\*

I could not talk to Dylan for months. Every time he tried to touch me, he felt like a stranger. It took me only a few days to move the rest of my trinkets from his place to my old one and settle back in for good. My place was so damn cold in every way.

I shook at the thought of Dylan, and of her. Everything that was her was him as well. All I could think about was

how much I wanted a baby. And not just that, I wanted a
girl. My girl. I needed to replace her.

The hurt felt so different because only he and I, and
the girl at the doctor's office, had ever known I'd been
pregnant. I had to grieve her in secret. And then I'd feel
bad about keeping it a secret. When Dylan tried to talk to
me, I blamed him. He took it, and he left me alone. He
was resilient at first until he just... wasn't. One day, he
got tired of "taking my sadness," and I heard him speak
in a deep voice into the side of my cheek, his breath
heavy and long as it held me against the wall:

"Lalanii, I lost just as much as you did. I lost her too."
His voice cracked when he spoke.

I was gonna tell Mama that week, then my sister, but then she was gone. My little girl was gone before anyone knew she was going to exist. I was going to tell them sooner, but there was so much of me that felt shame. Shame for going back to someone who was right for me in most ways except he was morally bankrupt, shame for admitting I'd accepted less just to be loved, shame for admitting I was scared to do this life alone— financially and emotionally—and surely shame I'd wanted someone so much it made me do radical things.

He said we could try again. He said we could get married and do things the "right way." He said we could get it all back. He said he just needed a little more time to give me everything. But some part of me knew Dylan

would never give up his profession. I spent the first week

afterward in shock and the next five in awe. Dylan and I

had dated so long, and I'd prioritized him so much, I

realized I didn't have very many friendships I'd kept up

outside of him. His happiness was my sole priority

because I'd felt so much that mine was his.

Dylan begged me to move to New York with him and

start over. It didn't work the first time I went to "try it,"

and it wouldn't work this time. New York was no place

for my son, and I'd have no help with him there. I was an

LA girl, born and raised in sunshine and overpriced lattes.

I was a beach mom—dragging my son to Venice

boardwalk to buy cheap sunglasses and knickknacks. He'd skateboarded or strolled alongside me, wearing shoes with wheels inside them. I couldn't see my life in New York. I couldn't imagine how my life would've blended with this man I loved so hopelessly I lost words to say.

*Shit happened*, once again.

I couldn't stop believing my baby girl didn't make it to this world for all the reasons I'd prayed I'd never gotten pregnant before. For all the missed pills and for the pills I took twice in a day trying not to get pregnant when I'd dated Liam.

For all the moments I'd begged my body:

"Please, not this time, ok?"

My body had answered.

# RESILIENCE

I'd taken a two-week assignment and buried myself in it. I was so sad I didn't even consider what Dylan was going through. I took his calls daily and breathed on the phone for about twenty minutes; each time, I said nothing. He eventually started to call less and less. This went on for a while. The assignment I had went full time and permanent because the previous senior copywriter got pregnant and decided not to come back to work. My colleagues gossiped next to the coffee machine that the former copywriter's husband was going to take care of her. I couldn't be sure who they were talking about, but it had to be the woman I'd replaced.

I could write 111 SKUs of copy into an Excel sheet in eight to nine hours, with over 90 percent correct, on their first run before editing. As much as it felt freeing to work for my own money and to have scored a gig I was proud of, I wanted nothing more than to be a mom again. I didn't see daylight. I was stuck in a glass cage with floor-to-ceiling windows behind a big white desk with double computer screens. Months and months and months glazed over. I cried in the bathroom and during lunch breaks in my car, and I cried in the shower. I would scream in a pillow for three hours sometimes. It wasn't the sadness that was killing me; it was the story of what could have been that kept playing. It was always that story, and I was writing it every day I thought about her. Until I came to

the conclusion that I just had to try hard not to think of it
because:

#1. The only thing I was losing now was my own time.

#2. My daughter, for this man, was not supposed to exist.

#3. This was my story, and I had to keep writing it.

Since then, Him #4 and I kept in touch maybe two or
three times a year. The weekend I found out he was
getting married to someone else, we'd been separated
from seriously dating for way more than a few years, and
I was seeing someone else. I was in Miami for my
birthday. A mutual friend slipped and mentioned his
engagement party to me when he'd called to give me

well-wishes. That friend must have called and let him

know he'd messed up the "bro code." After seventeen

missed calls from him, I read the text apologies and

deleted them as fast as I could. Finally, I answered.

 "All I want to know is why you didn't tell me

yourself?" I said into the phone with intention.

I wasn't angry. I was relaxed. I sat in my panties and a

tiny tee, two glasses into a bottle of white wine with my

mom on a balcony overlooking The Strip. I wasn't upset

that he didn't tell me as much as I was upset at myself for

expecting him to behave any differently after so many

years. To not call incessantly like I was important again,

to make me realize I still cared—even if just a little. To

not treat me as though nothing had changed. I realized he still cared, possibly even more than the man I was then seeing. Dylan and I hadn't been dating, and we weren't even friends at that time.

"Here we go with this again—" he'd started, noise and chattering in his background telling me there were a lot of more important things he should've been doing.

"So you're calling me like this 'cause you're bored?" I had a bad habit of cutting people off because I was afraid of hearing anything they might say that could affect me before I'd made my point. I had a bad habit of listening only enough to be *right*, rather than listening for *understanding.*

He hung up.

A week later, I heard through the same mouthy friend that he'd called his engagement off. We haven't spoken since.

# RESILIENCE

I CAME OUT OF IT BUT BROKE ME.

NO ONE COULD BE TRUSTED.

Business Decisions

I'm not in love.

    I don't fall in love.

        I make business decisions.

           I make two-year plans and if you can't deliver,

I reroute without a tracking number so you can't reconsider.

Very few people could make it any more simple.

I tickle when I think about it. Really.

    I don't pout about it.

I just conjure up my will and POOF!

Into thin air. Like you never existed.

This is how I erase the years I spent with the wrong people.

I don't fall in love.

That tickling and twinkling giggles.

Winks and shimmery shining glistening.

Like a glowworm in the distance.

Whistling teapots but whispers gentle as simple mornings, rah-rah.

The can't stop thinking of you, even when I blink hard.

No. Not interested.

Six months queue Operation Care Less.

Regret piles up like laundry unfolded.

Morning breath smells of hail and cemetery.

No more lying in a hammock, spread-eagle naked,

cucumbers over eyes, fingertips sitting still on me.

No more nibbling nipples like shriveled-

sugared strawberries at attention.

Nope, not really.

This is love.

And you will love me until you're sick of me, then after
that, you will be miserable.

And all who are not interested say I.

i.

So you won't have my heartbeat on a bread of mistake for
breakfast.

You won't have to pretend to coddle me in honesty or
accept my "as-is" bullshit.

We won't have coordinating schedules, adjacent rules,
and regulations.

Or consequences pending eggshells or misplacement.

You don't have to worry about either of us having our meal replacement shakes and eating bad too. Because you're not going to love me and I'm not going to love you.

# CHAPTER 7

# PAIN

I only met Mike because I'd taken Dylan back. Mike had kids, after all. I thought he'd understand me more.

PAIN

BUT YOU'VE GOT TO BE CAREFUL

WHAT YOU WISH FOR.

One night, I decided to go out dancing, and I met Mike, Him #5. Well, technically, I drunkenly stumbled into Mike. I was too many drinks in, and I fell— *shoulders first*—into him. I began shouting at him about where my friend was.

"I have no idea where your friend is!" He turned to face me, his expression pure joy. I could see him checking me out.

He stood about five foot eleven—like he could have been the spawn of Swiss Beats and Common, if they'd had a baby together. Bald head, super-beautiful smile, built arms (but not too big at all), and the best part? He

was disarming. He reminded me of an almond butter–
colored Popeye.

\*

I was an awkward introvert stuck hiding inside of an
extrovert personality. I needed to get out. Each part of me
needed to relearn how to be alive again, and I was unsure
of how to do so. Feeling alive had a lot to do with what
you allowed yourself to let go of.

I decided to let go of my pride and fear and call up the
one party guy I knew. The best way to forget (at least
temporarily) was to distract and deflect. The conversation

went like this: *Hey, what's up, you know of a lot of clubs and stuff, right?* We went out there. After a night in VIP, being hit on left, right, and from the side, me and my party guy friend ended up at an After Hours club. I'd never been to any club like that before, so this was all new. I discovered later, from other people there, that the party guy I attended this party with did lots of cocaine. I didn't know that at the time.

I might have responded inaccurately when they offered me some. "Oh, no, no, I don't smoke—hurts my lungs," I said as cool as I could. The guy laughed and whispered to his friend. I didn't even know what to look for as signs of a drug user.

\*

So that was the night I ran straight into Mike. He and I sobered up quickly and started talking about our kids. Really. I'd been to clubs, house parties, and shindigs. But never this setting. The fluorescent tables shone bright—colors morphing unlike anything I'd ever seen. He said he had two teenage daughters. At that exact moment, I knew. He could understand me as a mother—him being a father—in a way that Dylan never could. As he told me about his little girls, I forgot about Dylan for the first time in I couldn't remember how long. I forgot about my dead baby girl and my abusive ex-boyfriend. I forgot about my attack, I forgot I was a single mom, I forgot—I forgot about all the people who hurt me, I forgot all of that, and

then, I remembered laughing so hard I got the hiccups.

## Wildflowers

"But how should I court you?"

"Wildflowers," I tell him.

"Wildflowers and caramel dripping from the edges of the
nonfiction you read me.


Watch with me, turtledoves floating by

sell me your spiel, point at the ducklings

show me why you laugh on a morning with no color but
cerulean


carry me to a lost moon, near a wet drain

explain to me that a ladybug met a bumblebee one day

and they made love in a garden of pink petunias and

orange chrysanthemums


and tell me they flitter-sting

and that you will sing me a song

with light like a dim house as it snows


kiss me on the harbor until you run out of words

then ask me to guide you and compare how that works

against knowing everything you don't


and how that catches a pinch of this rainbow,

plops it into your coffee cup at 6:14 a.m.

and starts this poem over."

A few weeks later, Mike invited me to his house to watch the football game. I called everyone I knew because I didn't want to go alone. I'd never been into sports, nor liked football, but an old homegirl and I went. From there, Mike and I began dating. Every week, a new spot—just to show off. Drinks. Dinners. I'd get a whole new outfit and shoes just for him to parade me around in. From football Sunday earlier that year extending through Memorial Day weekend, and then beyond, we got to know each other; we really dated.

I was 160 or so pounds when we met... down from the 183 I'd been a few months prior, but I was still quite heavy for my height—barely hitting five feet without heels. I'd gained so much weight being sad.

That was when I hired a trainer and then a nutritionist, but it wasn't until I'd thought about whether I would physically desire me at my current state that I decided to take them both seriously. If *I* didn't want me, Mike wouldn't want me either. I wasn't about to feel the type of chemistry I hadn't felt in forever—and then lose it over something I could do something about. In a few weeks, I'd hit 140 pounds working out twice daily five to six times a week with my trainer. I paid close attention to everything I ate.

I'd lost a total of forty-three pounds because I'd found something or rather *someone* who'd motivated me to believe I was worth enough to do it all—*for me*. I also had to admit I did it *for him.* The inspirational push I felt knowing he supported my weight loss endeavors while also eating healthy (with me) was all I needed to stay on track.

But then, something started to happen as summer approached, and I worried he was going to "friend-zone" me. We hadn't even kissed or had sex, and it was more than five months. I tried to decipher the relationships I'd

had to see why it wasn't progressing and if there was
anything I could do:

&ast; With Henry… I was so young, I didn't know any
better anyway.

&ast; With Evan… No matter if I wanted to admit it or
not, I'd been victimized.

&ast; With Liam… I'd been controlled mentally and
abused physically.

&ast; With Dylan… I was lied to. I'd been emotionally
paralyzed by fear and loss.

&ast; With Mike… It was like I was being bamboozled. It
was like he was scared to love me at all, so I had to do all

the work. Strangely, the relationship only ever had my efforts—efforts that would carry us into the years we had, but only as long as I was ok to carry us.

May came, and we still hadn't slept together, but we'd been consistently talking for hours on end. One night, we went to a karaoke bar. I ordered two shots and asked him if he was gay—he had female tendencies, after all, and he was a good listener. It would have been fine for us to stay friends. I just didn't want to waste more time not knowing for sure if he were gay or married. Mike treated me like I was an undiscovered coin worth a bajillion dollars. It was *just* too good to be true, according to a few people I told about him.

Moments later, Mike flagged the waiter down by doing the neck-slash hand movement known as "kill everything you're doing and close me out."

That night, we fucked until we made love, and we made love until we fucked. I was sore and raw, and it was terrible at first, but by the third time, he had it exactly right, and it turned out lovely. He slowed down, he sped up, and then we fell in sync like a wave came, and we both caught it, then relaxed in it. It was the first time I ever had to call off work. There wasn't enough money in the world that would've made me leave that bed.

Six weeks later, I graduated from my master's
program with a dual-concentration creative writing
degree.

When people used to see us so happy and ask us what
the secret to "us" was, we'd both tell them we never went
a day without talking. Not one day.

I realized I'd never had anyone believe in me in that
way, so to have someone believe in me was a bond I
thought could never be broken. It was a journey in a
specific order: If I hadn't taken Dylan back and lost our
child together, I never would have met Mike, who was a
father already. I hadn't dated anyone who'd had kids, and
I felt that was one of the main reasons why he and I

would work. He already knew what it was like to be someone's father; he wouldn't misplace his life or put himself in danger the way Dylan would. Or so I thought.

If I hadn't been so broken, I wouldn't have met Mike. I might have met someone at a bookstore or a Target or a networking event. I would have met someone less wound up. I wouldn't have gone out self-medicating via vodka cranberry, barely able to handle two in a row. Maybe who I would have met would've been more stable. But I never would have met someone like him. Like, ever.

Mike had this grow house with lamps and all, right in his garage, and he lived in a house with his business partner/ex-girlfriend—which, yes, was weird already—

but I would get used to it, he assured me. I later learned they'd dated long-term for more than twelve years, which was how she became the "sister." I never got used to it.

He was a "boy version of me," I would brag to my family in the beginning. They had only ever heard of Dylan, but with Mike, my family got the *This Is The One Speech* before we'd even slept together. He was outgoing but soft tempered, an effortless blend of high energy but low key. He was described most easily as… *fun*. He lived in Leimert Park, a beautiful area in Los Angeles.

I had somewhat regular working hours; his workdays were fourteen-to-eighteen-hour days or more—"but great money," he bragged. We talked on the way to work, and we talked on the way home. It became hard to go to sleep without him. I discovered his work hours weren't enough time together since he got off so late. I wouldn't get to see him unless he spent the night.

The grow house garage failed miserably because he forgot to water and care for it. I laughed at his loss because it wasn't a big deal to me when it should have been. Moreover, I laughed at him, letting go of his responsibilities—*for me*. We had sex every single night, and if we got a break, we missed one night—maybe. It was my-house-then-his-house-sleepovers for a while until we both decided it wasn't so great to keep leaving my preteen home alone; so then, he started to stay at my house each night. This was why he forgot to water his plants.

*

I was in this world alone, but I never told anyone just how alone I felt. The more Mike got to know me, the more he liked to remind me of how many "true friends you do not have." I'd made this choice after realizing a lot of people around me could be unsafe or not trustworthy. By this time, Mama and her side of the family had long since moved to the East Coast (Richmond, Virginia) as she had three other grandchildren. They'd moved two relationships ago, back when Liam and I first got engaged, she couldn't afford

LA. Mama was sure I'd be fine, even though she'd really

just done what was best *for her*.

# PAIN

I WASN'T FINE. BUT I DIDN'T HAVE THE

OPTION TO NOT BE... FINE.

Him #5 moved in.

## Trying

I'm trying to love you but Mom's a drunk

Dad's losing his house and there isn't any of me left.

I'm trying to love you but the man I loved most was

doubtful

I think he would sprout with a pinch of garlic salt.

I'm trying to love you but I'm out. All out.

I'm ruling house, but I already gave up the numbers.

I'm trying to fail up.

I'm spiraling downward.

The whole house is indifferent and all we did

Was break each other better than it ever could have been.


If I weren't Wish Proof, you'd have been my first wish.


\*


    Culver City Arts District started to boom right then.

Our weekly outings were walkable—I lived right next to

the studios. One of the best times I can remember was

when we'd met a couple out. They courted us both all

night, buying us drinks, the woman swooning over him,

the man's eyes on me. We gave each other side-eyes,

knowing we were going home together. These types of

"secrets" used to make me feel so close to him. At the end of our "free night," the couple that had been all over us both advanced on us individually. We were left scrambling, looking for a way out of their proposals for "heading back to your place." We ended up walking home side by side, laughing hysterically while imitating their attempts. I described the man's shoes; he told me in detail about the woman's all-too-forward nature and terrible teeth and breath. Good times.

It was more than convenient to be able to go out and walk home. Once, we'd actually dropped our clothes at the door like they do in movies. We made love to Beyoncé's "Crazy in Love"—oh, we went on for hours.

Another time in the middle of the night, I was mid-orgasm when I mistakenly pushed one of our bed accent pillows into a candle. Romantic, *I know*. The flame blazed up high from the nightstand. I hopped up in sheer fear, raising my hands up and down like a lunatic while he struggled to smother the fire, all in the buck. I'd done nothing to assist, but I still—to this day—will swear on my life I'd never laughed as hard. He'd say the same.

There were so many times like this. I remember them as the years passed, even though as the time went by, they lessened. I saw them like the movies we used to spend hours discussing. It got to a point where he could know

the specific bar I'd go to after my long day, and it'd go
like this:

 "So what you 'bout to do?"

"I don't know, these clients, I had a day, man. I'm
prob'ly just 'bouta go home," I'd tell him.

"Oh, are you?" he'd say.

Hours later, we'd wind up at that same bar. Again
catching eyes across the room as we entertained other
people, smiling. What was "cute in the beginning"
usually turns out to be not so damn "cute" as the
relationship progresses—but you can't convince anyone
of this; it has to just backfire. He'd walk up to me, and I

would fall in love eleven times over. It wasn't so much flirting with others as much as it was *us*. Us as conversationalists. The one thing I knew we had in common was our love for conversing with people over drinks.

Well… that was the story I told myself.

\*

At year two, we hit *sticky*. I guess I just figured it'd all work out. I used Mike's daughters as a measurement of the type of guy he was. The time he spent with them wasn't plentiful, but from what I could tell, then, it was favorable.

A broken family was all he knew, so without miraculous efforts (I should have seen the signs), a broken family was all he'd ever have. After a year and a month or so of him spending the night at my house, my job contract ended abruptly. In his defense, he still had his place and could go home whenever he wanted. But we didn't want that. We faced the inevitable conversation of him needing to *finally* chip in financially.

## Suspension of Unconsciousness

I want proof I want hard swimming
I want a comeback like it rules the whole kingdom
I want havoc in habit
I want the decorations to be envy green
I want the way it forgets to be the way it's remembered
But I want to just not do it
I want the patience to go beyond the splendor
I want proof I want hard factual caffeinated qualitative
The further it is the closer I get
I want my slow hours back the code words
The debt and doubt, the high-lows
I want the whole enchiladalasagnapastameringue with
butter cheese baked
and I want the doorbell to ring
letting go of three dozen floating I'm so sorry balloons

For being a buffoon I tell you a buffoon I tell you a
bombastic lunatic
Licking the eyelids of lament
I want the proof to show up even when it's written in
clear print
Like the freezing breeze at 5 a.m.
Like the sweating dreams, lucky ducky shucks me
I want it washable. I want it variable. I want it falling off
Like a lucky star in the middle of a broken-winged
catastrophe
Air writing of my name. My name. My name in
somebody's sky
Good-er than whistling walking backwards with my
thoughts not listening
I want to pucker when I'm in a certain zip code
Ruffle up my shoulders. Snuffle up my nose and shot
eyes and
I want proof like a consistent sniffle

I want autopilot off

A shorter commute

I want a new window view

# TIME

Not that you asked, but the state of Him #5 and I's relationship the year after that next one—not so peachy either:

Tolerance. Hopelessness. Brevity. Boredom. Stuck. *Sticky.* The man I'd loved bigger than a tsunami was a liar and a workaholic and made me feel like leftovers. Not same-day leftovers. The kind you forgot about and then you open the fridge, and you're like, *I'd better eat this, it's only got one day left. Sticky* was when two people loved the heck out of each other but really needed to figure out if a *sticky* situation was what they wanted to work through. *Sticky* was silky quicksand. *Sticky* was stuck-sinking. More than likely, *sticky* had 30 percent chances—at best.

At the end of our second year, two counselors told us we had no chance. They told us that we were two very different individuals who were awfully set in our ways and beyond compromise. We ignored them both. Nothing worth it in life or love was to come easily. He was, after all, the man I'd wished for. The guy I imagined with no face who waited at the altar… as I floated down in my powder-puff dress. The one who was more my best friend than anyone had ever been. The one who would have given me the daughter who would have made it.

But the best definition for *sticky* was this: finding out the man you loved like a whirlwind swirling had impregnated a woman in a different state, and because it'd happened before you started seriously dating, he didn't tell you. A woman who'd told him she couldn't get pregnant but who then gave him a two-for-one special. Twin boys.

When Mike told me he didn't want any more children, later in our relationship, I didn't believe him because I still clung to what he'd said to me on our first date. We sat face-to-face on an evening under a blue streetlamp glow, talking beyond their closing hours. The Tender Greens workers left us cold on the patio. The red wine made me ask if he would have any more children even before I asked if he ever wanted to be married.

"For my wife, yeah, I could have one more," he told me. Our eyes stopped at each other. Stuck and glued into a long pause.

"I've never, like, raised a child—in the same house as their mother—so I guess I could see myself doing that," he mumbled, looking away. My heart jumped. It was the first date, but still, he wanted another child! Our little girl would be beautiful, I thought.

*Sidebar:* About five months after that glass of red and a week or so after us making what I thought at the time was love… he told me he needed to say something to me, so I should sit down on my white pleatherette couch.

I sat.

He explained that the doctors did a swab test, and he was having a baby. That's when he confessed there was another gal he'd impregnated on his way to destruction. They'd apparently connected on a spiritual level: between the church and her legs, so their son together would be only a few months old at the start of our relationship.

When Him #5 and I were moving from my house into a house we'd share together with our kids, he'd counted and thrown away over eighteen or so large trash bags filled with blankets and comforters.

Years and years later… in the week we were breaking up, as I was moving out of the second house we'd lived in together, I remember taking very few blankets and covers. This was so I could measure by count of blankets how happy I was, or rather, how much I was still trying to fix by "making it prettier."

That week, he told me the mother of his twin boys was getting married to someone. This was a woman he described as filled with angst, futile, raunchy, petty, and undesirable at every level. The woman who held over $30,000 of back child support over his head as bait while he pleaded with her every few years to make a deal. If he defaulted, he could lose his license. This back support would go to the county, the money he failed to pay when he was younger—so she would not see this money—but yet she failed to make the deal for $5,000 or even $10,000. Once, he told me he conceded paying her off as much as $15,000. She'd gotten him and an attorney down to the offices, the entire family in tow—and she made a huge scene and backed out. I heard stories his friends told me of him becoming so angry at her that he'd once physically punched her in her stomach. This woman, who I knew only by his absolute disgust with her, was *getting married*.

If that weren't enough, he'd also had another child in *another* state with a woman who had already married someone else. The story he told me was that she'd called one day to ask if her husband could legally adopt his little girl, and he'd given the child away like a Frisbee on sale. If one of his friends hadn't gotten drunk on a boat that summer with us hollering out about him having five-to-*six* kids, I would have likely never known. He showed me one blurry picture of her—once. This child was caramel colored with a big smile and dark hair and looked like the little girl we could have made. I started to resent him for everything I'd found out so slowly—it was too late to stop how I felt by now.

One night, after he'd been drinking, he confessed the reason he'd taken so long to be intimate with me when we first met was that he'd still been sleeping with his ex. Not too long after that, the same ex showed up at his daughter's graduation in the same week I'd walked in on him speaking to her over the phone inappropriately. I was not like him, and he was not the "boy version of me." No, I'd been wrong.

Mike and I stopped acknowledging our relationship except to our closest friends and family because he'd pitched me this awfully great idea (I believed at the time) that I was "building a brand." He'd gone on about how it looked better for me to be single, you know, for more supporters. When we went out, we never held hands or appeared as a couple in any capacity. Me appearing single meant he would also always appear single and therefore act as such. This also meant we would develop a more in-depth level into our "situationship," which was his way of "supporting my mission" but staying entirely out of it. This didn't create much of anything other than a sinking feeling and overwhelming mistrust.

I grew more and more insecure about us.

We grew apart.

By year four, I wanted to stop going out with him... but we didn't have anything else in common. All I could remember was how many times we'd gone out and "gotten into it," whether it was his friends screaming at me, him not standing up for me, or just me having an all-around terrible time around him. At that time, we were having sex once a week, if that.

Making money came first to him, which had always been true—but now, he began to make it clear I wasn't the one by not inviting me out and not including me in the secret worlds he created. His job became this place where he cultivated work-ships that pushed along his alcohol and drug habits. He would come home to report that he'd found yet another "woman" he could coerce into thinking he *actually liked* or wanted a friendship with, so they could schedule him for additional work. He was in the entertainment industry, so this was to be expected. Perhaps maybe his job didn't *become* this place, but rather, it was *always* this place for him, and what changed was his willingness to care about my feelings or mask his experiences or overall morals. He began to tell me about befriending people in the name of networking so he could stay booked on jobs, always busy, and when I asked him if he actually cared about the friendships he'd made, he sometimes wouldn't even remember them. He made sure to mention that they *always* remembered him, however. He was handsome, after all.

At first, I was ok about this. It meant no one actually *meant* anything to him, it was a numbers game… I still meant everything to him. But, later, when he'd take phone calls during the dinners I made for him, check texts midconversation, and create reasons to go out without me—but invite me because he knew I wouldn't accept the invitation because of how I'd been treated before—I got weary. If we went out, he'd set me up to have an awful time, so that way, he could go out willingly and not come home until the next day, or two, and I wouldn't think I was missing a thing. I got numb; *everybody* meant something to him, but I wasn't special at all.

One of the last few times we went out, he got so drunk he choked me in his parked car in Santa Monica after a club. I don't remember what we argued over, but he snapped out of it fast enough and apologized, and he never put his hands on me again. I knew it was only that one time, however. Liam used to have a few months of "good behavior" as well. The trouble with having gone through a lot was that everything became a trigger. Everything I experienced became a reminder or a red flag. Apologies meant nothing, and heartbreak was a side effect of love. Heartbreak was not something love came without for me.

Before that, we'd had the usual drunk escapades with his friends, and they'd all ended in absolute disaster.

One night, one of the drunk gals in his crew was scream-spitting in my face about how Mike was *not going home with me* and how I needed to *get the fuck on.*

I remember leaving The Shack in Playa Del Rey in an Uber, unable to even speak to the driver—I was in such shock.

Another time, we'd all been drinking, and I'd mistakenly confided in his business partner/ex about borrowing money from one of *my exes*. Right then, she'd attempted to fight me, her arms swung wide.

"How dare you put Mike in danger you biiiitCHhHHhHH!" his ex screamed as she lunged at me, her friends catching her, holding her from me. No one had been in any danger. Alcohol can bring out imminent feelings and paranoia. She was the last of his friends to do something foul to me. There was just no more

forgiveness left in me, no more try. The commotion was
raunchy and roared through the already not-so-super-
great area, and I was scared. Confrontation triggered even
more fear for me. I ran to my car and sped off. I shook,
trying to hold the steering wheel steady. I paid my ex
back, but I never forgot the ordeal. The business I tried to
start with the money he'd lent me had failed. I needed
support to grow it while still maintaining it—only then
could it have survived. His business partner/ex eventually
got married to a guy she met in half the time Mike and I
had been together. I wasn't invited, nor did I want to go.

On another drunk night in Hollywood, we'd had a
fight in front of everyone. He called me out of my name

once again. One of his guy buddies quickly had me in a stranglehold while his brother screamed out obscenities and the ex-bouncer-gangster-looking guy barely let me go in enough time for me to scream and run down the street barefoot in and hop in some nice gay couple's car. I begged them to drive me home even though I had no money and only a purse strap—no purse, just a phone. They took me home willingly. Five minutes into the ride, I was screaming a Britney Spears song with them.

I finally knew. I loved Mike so much I still saw the good in him, and against my better judgment, I put him before myself.

TIME

LESS TO DO WITH LOVING SOMEBODY.

MORE TO DO WITH

LOVING SOMEBODY IN THE

RIGHT WAY.

I continued to accept Him #5's ways as a sort of realization that everyone had to "go through shit." All I'd seen were the people I loved "going through shit." It was the way I thought love was supposed to be; it was the standard my romantic world (as I knew it) was built from. I learned to respond to his behaviors less and less because the more I did, the more I would actually "feel" something, and *the more it would hurt*. If we argued about a trust issue and couldn't find a solution, I'd inadvertently learn from that argument that he couldn't be trusted. Once I'd learned the same thing a few times, it was so. I eventually stopped arguing about everything altogether. It was a brilliant coping mechanism until I realized it had grown to indifference, and there was nothing that separated him from a stranger to me.

I stopped calling him in the mornings before work, and I didn't call him after. Since I'd always been holding up the relationship, if I didn't do those things, he wouldn't either. I began to refer to him as an on-and-off, a roommate, and even, at times, "my homeboy." That's what he became to me.

It took many years to realize I'd loved him so much it made me dislike him. I disliked the person who he had always been—the person he hid. Addicted to stimulation, addicted to response, *addicted*.

I knew then that a lot of people had mental, emotional, or physically traumatizing stories. Even still, given those experiences... what I craved most from the person I loved was to not be led around an idea or given a false reality. I wanted to be given a *choice* when most everyone had a representative standing in front of who they really were. I wanted to be kept in the loop as things changed.

Most people don't communicate their traumas, openly display fears or issues, or share experiences. Talking about these things builds understanding. Once Mike and I lost understanding, we lost. As people, we don't get to choose the physical appearances we are born with. We are also unable to choose our mental or emotional states unless we're aware of them by learning more about them—often, not even then. And yet, looks, emotional intelligence, and ways of thinking coupled with personality were all driving forces in who we were attracted to and why. After almost nine years, I'd been sleeping next to a person I did not even know.

Mike kept up his drunken stupors, and one night we had a fight (not unusual), and he took his piggy bank (an oversized plastic Heineken bottle filled with bills and coins) to a 7-Eleven. When I found him the next morning, he was naked except socks on our bedroom floor with teary red eyes, confessing he'd mistakenly left his full piggy bank at the corner store, and it had anywhere

between $2,000 and $4,000 of crumpled bills and change
inside. Everything came back to how well we knew each
other and how much we trusted each other. It all came
back to the understanding we no longer had of each other.
I asked him blankly why he even took it with him and if
he thought I was going to steal from him. He couldn't
answer. He'd fallen asleep.

# TIME

WE OFTEN CONFUSE

WHAT WE WISH FOR WITH WHAT IS.

-NEIL GAIMAN

## Wish Proof

I walked upside wrong begging for air on your moon.

I tossed, I turned, and I learned this:

I sold myself a loss to sell myself what it cost me—it wasn't a good idea to love you.
I'd cook you anything you asked me, all you had to do was ask me.

You got drunk and everything—everything got haunted in you.
I guess, baby, maybe, maybe I'm just wish proof.

I wished it so bad I couldn't dream it bigger than you.
I would've given up anything. Anything for you.

I blew kisses in wishes to grant us our wish lists you rode in on a white unicorn with a flask—sparkling rosé and a wand and said—YOU.

I flew a carpet, rubbed a genie, watched the sand slip slip through the hourglass, and I watched you laugh with your fuckin' friends at my expense.

I saw you not give a damn about me, except where you spent it.
Showing off till you were blue.

And yeah maybe you believed in me but not as hard as I believed in YOU.

I fought my demons I fought yours. I gave up dreams I shouldn't have had to.
Tell me you were faithful we can beat the dead horse to the grave enough to show you I'm truly grateful but we have nothing left 'cause you're greedy and hateful.

And time trumps money—I don't have enough time left to wish on you.

Maybe I loved you too much and left nothing but loose ends.

I loved you so much I didn't leave anything left for you to do.

Maybe, baby I'm, I'm just Wish Proof.
You know… we win some… some we lose.


Without any warning a few weeks later, Mike called and abruptly said the following:


"Babe, I'm checking myself in. They're gonna take my phone—you'll have to tell everybody I'm ok; I'm at Exodus, it's the rehab, in Culver City. I'll call you back when they let me have a phone call."

I was confused. I collapsed into the couch, burying my face in my hands. I didn't know the severity of his drug use and certainly didn't expect for it to have spiraled enough to check into any hospital.

\*

Bright yellow walls matched the color of crazy. Not too far from the way the pastel yellow I'd wanted in the nursery for my daughter drove me crazy to see it after she was gone. It wasn't the color; it was the associated memory. I saw that bright yellow with white trim, and I froze. As I stepped off the elevator, I saw his face, and I could tell whatever they'd given him caused a few seconds of confusion as it took him a bit to recognize

who I was. He looked shallow in his eyes, and his posture

was sunken. It had only been three days. The thing I

wasn't ready for when he checked himself in was that

hospitals don't differentiate between addiction and mental

illness, which meant all I saw around him were people

talking to those yellow walls. People screaming their hair

was on fire—no noticeable fire. And men walking into

feeding tables as their pants fell down at their knees. I

went every visiting hour they would let me in. I called

that hospital until I knew the number by heart. I scream-

cried into the mattress on his side of the bed each night he

was gone, but I showed up to the hospital with a strong,

nonchalant smile. I saw one of his brothers there once,

and according to him, he'd been his only visitor and only came that once.

Mike told me that he'd confided in the staff, saying that once he started drinking, voices told him he could have another drink or just one pill. Then one became one more, and so on. They sent him home after more than three weeks with pills for bipolar disorder. I looked up the medications and threw them in the trash. His mom already had bipolar disorder—I didn't want to chance it.

He left rehab with classes to attend once or twice a week. There, he met a female friend, and he told me he hung out with her regularly. I was more than the fool when a year after he cut her off, he told me he'd cut her out because they'd done a few lines together. So, essentially, he'd met his addiction with someone else's addiction and fed his addiction while shutting me out for not accepting him as he was. The girl he met at rehab was no different than the other friends he hid from me. Later, at a family function, I saw some of his family members doing drugs too. Basically, he was doomed.

"What outcome could you have expected?" One of my friends asked me once. I had no answer then, but let me tell you:

You cannot love addiction out of anyone

because he would have surely been cured.

\*\*\*

Years later, he went to Europe because one of his best friends was getting married there. I found out a day or so before he left. He lied, pretending he couldn't afford it and that his friends paid for his ticket and all expenses. He gave me detailed explanations when he "checked in," explaining how he was completely broke and couldn't even "pay for any of my meals." He joked about this to me at every restaurant or event while touring all of Europe for nearly three weeks. To go to Europe was then and had always been a dream of mine.

That was his last trip out of the country before he had to surrender his then-expired passport due to unpaid back child support; it caught up with him. I would have loved the experience, but he didn't know that because he didn't take the time to continue to know me. Or he did know that much, which was the reason he'd jumped through so many hoops to be sure I knew he couldn't possibly afford to take us both. More than likely, the bride and groom didn't care for me much, as he consistently repainted our negative storyline while denying he did so. I didn't mind him or me not being able to afford a vacation for *us*; what I found hurtful was thinking back about how he'd pretended he wasn't going out of town, and then him

instantaneously getting packed and being gone. It was…
the secrecy.

I went on like nothing he'd done mattered because
every time we tried to discuss anything, it'd end up in an
argument or the silent treatment for days. I just didn't
want the inconvenience. We shared a bed together. Sleep
was important, I told myself.

Me not going to Europe with him was the last straw in
the last mixed drink we'd ever not have together again. I
don't think from that point on that there was anything he
or I could have done to repair the social damage his antics
had caused to our relationship, and still, *I tried.*

His other friend had a bachelorette party in Mexico, and he invited me. I shouldn't have gone. I knew better, but it was a different environment, and I longed for what a vacation could do for us—even if celebrating someone else. About 2.5 hours in, he'd already gotten drunk and began to chuckle loudly about how I didn't suck his dick to match the bachelorette party penis straws we all sipped from. There were a few other comments he said under his breath, and even his friends were uncomfortable. I left with red cheeks trying to catch a taxi from Rosarito, completely clueless—touristy and alone—with two expensive-looking bags, a backpack, and a laptop in tow. I likely paid three times the price for cash tips and services. Not one of my friends answered when I called, so I ended up getting picked up by his youngest daughter and her boyfriend. When I finally got home, I took a hot shower and cried myself to sleep. I'd been scared and humiliated yet again.

So what do you do when you give a man nearly a decade?

Just give up? Just walk away? I could do no such thing.

# TIME

"BE CAREFUL WHAT YOU ALLOW YOURSELF
TO GET USED TO. YOU CAN GET USED TO
ANYTHING." - DAD

Years of *no better* went by, and each morning before he'd leave, I'd snuggle over him, grabbing him from his side as he lay with his back to me. Once when I held him, my tears dripped from my eyes onto his bare skin. It was warm, and he'd worn no shirt to bed. We were surely roommates now because this was one of the few mornings he actually came home and woke up with me. He'd been saying he had "overnight jobs" too many times a month to make it believable by anyone.

Three nights before I moved out, he finally decided to ask me if I'd been crying.

"I have been crying over your back for such a long while now, every morning. You have just noticed this?" I said numbly.

What I wanted to ask him was: *"Have you ever watched somebody sleep? Have you ever wanted the best for someone even if you knew they wouldn't choose you? Have you ever grown apart when you wanted to grow through it? Have you ever had to choose someone else's happiness even if it meant you were going to lose entirely? Have you ever had to look yourself in the eyes and tell yourself the truth?"*

I had gotten so used to him; I could not imagine my life without him. There was none. I walked out of the room and took the silence with me.

My mother never read to me; she'd just said in her Southern accent, "Well, you just ain't had enough yet, honey, 'cause when you've had enough, you'll *do* something."

My dad never read to me; he just drew me pictures and told me stories I could choose to apply to my life, or not.

When one of my closest friends read early drafts of this book, she'd suggested that perhaps I became a better writer because I didn't grow up being read to all the time. She went on to explain that my voice was always raw and

rarely edited properly, always *different—distinctly me.*
Reading to me was something no one had ever done,
except in writer's groups. I was in love with language. I
was in love with words. Couldn't *anyone* have imagined
my love language? I had been with this man for almost a
decade; I was running out of time for my own dreams.

Mike had written to me maybe a handful of times in
all the time we'd spent together. If I had ever handed him
something to read, it would've taken him triple the
amount of time I took to read it, double the amount of
time to understand what he read, and at least a full five
minutes before he could extrapolate anything or apply it
to any thoughts of his own—let alone implementation.

Mike was, however, gorgeous. He didn't display a lot of emotional intelligence, but he was wholeheartedly aware. He underestimated me in a way that made me weaker, and he'd noted this often by reminding me of how "book smart" I was, as if to say that wasn't very smart at all.

I was talking about this book for years, and it changed into so many different versions of being stuck in reverse stop-motion. Would it be a memoir? Would it be self-help? Would it be poetry? Would it be a way to free myself from everything that hurt me? Couldn't it be all of those things? Couldn't I be anything I wanted to be?

I wanted a man who would make love to me, but not just in the physical sense. All I'd found was pecking birds and fearful fucking, never anything magical.

Each one of these relationships changed me. More piercings. Tattooed my torso. Constant workouts. I only knew how to feel the push. I did not know how to float, sunbathe, or sleep on the sand. Those things were not anything I'd ever learned how to do. I no longer expected connection, and the people I'd meet would at best be just an experience.

WHAT I REALLY WANTED WAS SOMEONE WHO

WOULD KISS ALL OF THE WISHES OUT OF ME

AND REPLACE THEM WITH PROOF.

I finally accepted the fail of our relationship because, at the time, everything else was failing. I had to assume a "let it all go" type of bravery or weakness. Every problem from love, career, confusion, health, fear, grief, and anger seemed to take over at that same time.

The bonds around me failed so often throughout my life, I began to expect them all to fail. It was much like the book I'd been writing, but I just could not finish.

Dreamcatcher

I'm up… and it's late.

Clearly the dreamcatcher is broken.

Which means my daymares forsake me,

Can you please be more open?

Speak more openly?

Be more of a gateway, instead of a foyer?

Make sunshine in a corridor.

I know you gotta love the process as much as the outcome.

They have hope kits for this.

A dream of me: dreaming you.

One part water—two parts heart and air elope.

Sighed so loud I woke up caring so much I could float away.

Fair chance to love me but you're still standing still…

Like a faraway star.

With some lie-awake feelings.

And wishing wells… be a well of wishing wells of you.

Come heavy, baby, the time is stuck.

Dreams caught in a spider web.

Send help.

Send laughter.

Send happy.

Please I'm begging, I need the help and I'm asking.

# CHAPTER 8
# THE COMPLETE MESS
# COLLECTION

Mike and I sat on our couch next to each other, far apart enough to be strangers, close enough to have been roommates, but nothing left to indicate we had ever been in love.

Yes, our place was nice, beautiful, three bedrooms, two baths. The patio I spent most of my savings on in our first year there ended up becoming a smoke patio for our teenagers. Two months after I planted forty-seven baby veggies, herbs, and flowers indoors, they were all thriving... little peek-a-boos out of the seedling starter trays. A month later, they'd all spoiled over, flopping to the sides, losing their luster. I'd either watered them to death or our central heating we left on trying to warm the entire house was their death—maybe both. I got the patio gate painted pastel and blinking dragonfly LED lights for the garden that never sprouted. I'd told myself, on his off days, we could garden together. What off days? Oh, the days he took off for other people more important—those off days he had. Off days for me—he didn't have those.

I always wished for too much or not enough. I always did too much or not at all. Just like salsa dancing, or road trips, or the hot air balloon we drove three hours for only to find out they foresaw rain. Only to later find out that it was just overcast and we could go up… only to get into the hot air balloon, excited as ever, only to find out it could hardly leave the ground. The guy said the wind was weird. It wasn't the wind. The hot air balloon ride was amiss, and we were presented with I'm sorries and a gift certificate we promised we would use. Wishful thinking. We never went back. It was one of the last efforts Mike made to keep us together.

The garden would have worked, I told myself, if I'd have had help, if I weren't the only one out there on all fours in the dirt. The only bit of the garden I managed to plant that grew fearlessly were blueberries and brightly colored wildflowers that ended up at the entrance of our house, not the back patio. One morning, a friend came by and saw me picking the berries off the thick plant, about to pop them into my to-go blender. She snatched it from me.

"That is poison!"

"What? What are you talking about?"

"Look." She shoved her iPhone in my face with a picture of my exact poisonous wildflower. Round blue berries hung from it surely, just not—blueberries. Go figure. I couldn't believe it. The only thing that ever grew feverishly from this damn house was poison. Every time it grew back, I told Mike to cut it down so my three-pound Maltese wouldn't get sick. It grew back faster than his imagination when he lied. After a while, I didn't have to ask him to cut the plant. I'd see it growing up like ivy, then, the next day, like he'd taken his frustrations out on it… it was down to dirt and a thick stump. It was always back, though. Always.

We lived 1.1 miles from the beach. But we'd only ridden our bikes to the beach twice in two years. I'd claimed the beach was my favorite place and that biking was one of my favorite things to do. The best memories I had in that place weren't ever actually in the house. I bought a hammock. I'd always wanted a hammock. Not only could I not sit still in it enough to keep it from falling over and me falling out, but I only got in it three times, total. Our place had bad plumbing and leaked all over the beautiful hardwood floors, buckling them. The landlord forgot to add rain gutters to the garage, so when it rained, I cried slow tears while pushing water out with a janitor broom.

"My Babe Cave is ruined, my Babe Cave *is ruined*!"

Mike said nothing. He just sloshed the water out and shook his head when I was buying water stoppers to prevent more water damage. My Babe Cave was just a fancy mistake for a place I could keep what he called "your junk" out of the way, so I could be less of the organized chaos I was. I never went out there to write like the plan was. Because "out there," no matter how pretty it was, became a garage of insignificant stuff. I felt Mike's thoughts—silently judging, imagining I'd become a hoarder just like my dad. Every time he came out to the garage, there were more cutesy little fancy items I'd bought trying to appease myself. I couldn't concentrate on writing when I was alone because I was so obsessed with my relationship not being or getting where I wanted it. I was too focused on being sure he was happy; I never got to know what would make me happy. This was the end. We weren't even friends.

This was around the same time my dad started to age rapidly. I was in denial, I didn't see him ailing, but he was aging, mid-eighties. We were closer than ever. Even still, I was truly alone. A person doesn't just need family; a person needs outlets, a support system. And as far as our relationship? Well, we would have had to make no changes in both of our initial efforts to keep the relationship as much of a priority to us as it was when we'd first met. Mike built an entire life outside of me; I couldn't do a thing about it. It didn't take a lot of time to

let it fall apart; it didn't take any time much after I
stopped trying. I'd given it a few months shy of a decade;
I was committed.

*

"In ten years, heck, let's just say five years, you wake
up… in your house, in a place. What will you see around
you? What tangibly would you have around you?" I sat in
our bed with him one morning as he ate his oatmeal,
inside the bowl his assorted nuts, his berries. He
crunched.

"Like, what, like if I see, like, my bed? Like, I see a nice place. I see my breakfast. I see…" he rambled a list of tangible unimportant things to me as I looked around at everything we had—that belonged to me.

He was a minimalist.

I kept stuff.

He could survive with nothing.

My eyes skimmed his face, looking for him to say anything, anything about why I should've stayed. For him to mention me, my dog—heck, if he'd just say the bed we were lying in—anything that would have indicated he envisioned us being together would have sufficed.

No reason to stay was an excellent reason to go.


A week later, he was standing over the sink, shirt off, rinsing a dish, his abs bulging. It was hard for me to see him and not get distracted, impatient, want him to want me naked like I wanted him. Like I craved his attention, I craved his quality time like a kid. To not want him to face me and hold my hand, to not want him to ask me about something going on, to not want him to share with me— well, this just was not possible. But that person wasn't him anymore. These days, he behaved like I wasn't there.

It was eating me the way mold grows, first hidden and then—all of a sudden—everywhere.

"Do you consider me a burden?" I asked him a second question, trying to sound natural and nonchalant.

"Yeah, I mean, nah, I mean in comparison to some of my friends' wives who don't work, don't help out with anything financially, not now. No, I don't think so now," he stuttered back to me.

So in the grand scheme of things, Him #5 did consider me a burden—but not when compared to *wives* of friends of his, who did nothing professionally. But since I wasn't his wife, and we cohabitated, I *was* a burden—but somewhat—inexactly. I couldn't stomach it. I was ignored, I was not going to marry him or travel the world with him, I most certainly wasn't going to have any babies of his, and lastly, he made me feel as though I was holding him back. There was not one thing in this relationship left *for me*.

Being too afraid to fail by myself was a learned behavior, and I had to unlearn it, I told myself. I wasn't dependent on anyone and had been doing quite fine in my sadness before I met Mike. I didn't want to leave, but he'd gone so emotionally blind he couldn't even see me. It would be tough financially, but waking up in five to ten years in bed with him not seeing I still existed would be worse. I would lose everything I wanted if I settled

for him.

YOU CAN ONLY

IMPROVE WHAT YOU CAN MEASURE.

BUT YOU MUST STILL MANAGE THE THINGS

YOU CAN'T MEASURE AND IMPROVE THE

THINGS YOU CAN'T MANAGE.

Mike and I had the same musical taste; we liked the same decor and food. I'd lived with him for so many years, and it felt so much like living by myself. This was both good and bad, which made it harder.

Circumstances made a mess of us, and we stopped living because we were trying to make a life. I was working freelance and full time simultaneously, still making a little under half of his salary. He put so much pressure on me making enough money; it's all he ever talked about. Soon, I found, no matter how many more successful positions I pitched and won, I just wasn't enough for him. He started to spend more time with his family, which was difficult considering he didn't see me as such, and that became clearer and clearer to me as we went on. He started to spend more and more time with certain people because they were in his industry and they could hire him. He used people, and I started to see him for who he was. I wondered if he would have used me if I'd had more of what he wanted. He wouldn't even have entertained the people he entertained if they couldn't in one way or another put money in his pocket. He made it his *mission* to make them happy in any way he could. He ordered them personalized gifts through my Amazon account and paying for it to priority ship so he could give it to them before the job he was on with them ended. Made sure he was there for their birthdays, reciprocated their invitations, showed up and showed out personally to their weddings, moving parties, trips, and considered them "family," without fail.

He prioritized things that brought him more work. Then came his friends. This was no different from the beginning; it was just that now, eight years later, I wasn't prioritized in that mix at all. We hadn't just grown apart; we had two completely separate lives.

"I didn't have to do anything else. I paid for the majority of our living expenses, that's enough," he'd said to me, staring down as we ate at a sushi restaurant weeks later. That week, he went to pick up his son one night and explained he spent time with him by cooking tacos.

"So, you made tacos for Madison too?" I asked of his latest baby mama, jealously.

Madison had a big forehead, much like mine when I met her, but she wasn't friendly. Her jealousy back then was a whole vibe. I remembered one of our first encounters: At a reunion for Mike's family back when I'd first met him, Mike chased my son all around the park. She looked on, holding her newborn son. I caught eyes with her, and it was only then that I understood just how much I wanted a family, not just *to have somebody's son.* She rocked her child, calmly, but I could feel her energy, and it was threatened.

Mike had gone over to see this child, Isaac, and made them both dinner in their new house Mike told me Madison had bought the year before. I couldn't remember when he'd last cooked me a meal or when we'd had a good date night, but by default, because his son lived with the mother of this child, he had to magic-up veggie tacos for his makeshift family.

He wouldn't show up for me any longer. But by default, the rules had changed; he had to show up for her. I wasn't his family, and we had no real family, and no amount of denial I had was going to make it so.

## CAPTCHA'D

{sigh}

The best part about me is my thoughts.
The worst part about me is my thoughts.

He say he love me, man I ran outta heart.
He say he love me, but he rips me apart.

He lie like a cough when he caught.
He captcha'd.

He know he got me, so I'm captive.
He won't let me stay in love, but he's absent.

How were we gonna make sense?
He thinks it's a cash bar.

I wasn't into his looks; I was into his thoughts.
He wasn't the man that I thought.

Not what I thought, because that guy had heart;
he didn't stand there on guard, he didn't stand there at all.

He shoulda fought for me.
{Man} He shoulda fought better.


He wouldn't support me or my dreams in the way that
made me see they mattered to him. And that... that was a
way to die too.

Somehow we were together, but we were on the wrong
track. Maybe someday, we'd turn around and find that all
the reasons we couldn't find before would suddenly be
there—wouldn't that be grand? Or would time have
destroyed one of us by then—or maybe both—no less.

"LOVING SOMEONE MEANS TAKING THE
RISK THAT THEY MIGHT FUCK UP YOUR
NICELY ORDERED LITTLE LIFE."

- MARK HADDON

Mike was all I had, and he knew so. Even still—I was truly alone. In a relationship, a person doesn't just need family; a person needs outlets, while still making each other a priority. Him #5 built a life outside of me, and I couldn't do a thing about it. It didn't take a lot of time to let it fall apart. I'd given him a few months short of nine years, but the last four of those years… we'd become, at best, just friends.

About three weeks after that burdensome conversation, the last of our house together was packed up in a U-Haul and was now back to being just mine. My bed, my blender, my "too much junk in the way." He'd said he'd be at work on my moving day, so I didn't expect to have any issues, but his job for that day got canceled. He left for the gym but conveniently got back just as the movers were packing up the last of everything. I got in my car. My fragile stuff was packed, sun baking, as was my three-pound dog, Notebook. I started the car up, but in seconds I took off from the driver's seat, burst open the front door again to catch him on the edge of the couch. I jumped into his arms like a football tackle and sobbed. It was like he was there waiting for me to say good-bye.

"I love you so so so so soooooooo much, babe, and I can't believe this is happening, but I love you. This is so hard."

"Yeah, it is. I love you too," he said into my ear, not a tear in his eye—just a dreary look on his face.

We both knew it was never going to be the same again.

He squeezed me heavily, then harder for a long while. I took a huge breath and ran back to my car. Both of my hands shook as I put the key in, and then more as I turned the steering wheel. I raised my closed fist to my mouth, and a stream of tears fell. I watched the U-Haul in my rearview with my new life in it turn the corner.

I couldn't love beyond the numbness. I was restless with it. I would have kept looking back at our letters like wishes. I would never have thrown any of it away.

He had only the mattress I left him to sleep on and no furniture except for the couches he planned to leave outside and the oversized TV he put on the wall. My son moved out with a roommate months prior. His daughter moved out the week after I did. The family I'd so graciously tried to hold together was gone.

## Restless

*After Bob Hicok's "Twins"*

He has a regret and he has the same regret and he has a regret without knowing what it means.

When the light is off she wept with her eyes wide open she slept, and they both put their heads to the pillow chest—anticipating that it might seem certain.

He says that when he thinks he sometimes speaks between a timepiece and a treasure chest and that there's only a moment of time before she sees that.

He says she wore a prettier dress on the day that they met, and on the day that they met, like a moth dressed in powder, he says and he says, like a moth dressed delicately in water. Yes.

He says she's restless in her legs and when they made love, the headboard second-guessed which he guessed danced the brown sugar right out of her moans.

He plays in her navel with caramel; she snickers, and she plays with the same thing when he leaves. She plays, but it makes her sniffle when he leaves.

He says I love you first in September, and she says she's loved him as long as she can remember, and they go along wondering, and she goes along, claiming she loves him while she is asleep in her own insipid life he grows her the loneliest kites.

He is in love with her wants and he wants a Once Upon A Time, which is like, Once Upon A Time he should get what he wants.

He has to come to reality and he has to come back down to reality right now.

He says she has to be patient and he says please baby have patience and she says yes and then rushes him to frustration as he lulls her into hesitation about her needing to be patient at all.

And he has a regret and she has the same regret and in that regret she is regretting what she regrets and he is regretting what she regrets.

Then she sleeps.

THE ONE: A FREE-WILLED FIGMENT OF MY

IMAGINATION. LOVES TO NO LIMIT,

COMPELLED TO NO ORDER. MADE OF

SPARKLING EYES, AND WISHFUL. MY

MATTERHORN.

I wish it had turned out so much different than how it did. I couldn't swallow the fact that how it started wasn't what we grew into. When I slept, I remembered the few times we had together, most turning out badly, but there were moments: Our snow trip where I'd swear he was good enough to ski the Matterhorn. But when I was awake, all I could remember was the trip to the snow where he left me, and I had to figure a way down the top of the ghost-white mountain—alone—scared for my life because I didn't want to ask him to hang around and teach me, because I didn't want to ruin his good time. Alone because asking his friends and family for help was awkward, and I'd needed him, and he should've known that. He'd eventually taught me on the bunny slopes, but I never went back to the snow or river or any vacation with him. The fact was, I didn't want to be awake with him; all I wanted was the dreams I'd had for us. The dreams I'd thought we'd had.

I remember sitting on a bar patio in those last months with Mike and his friends. Two pills etched with numbers slipped from his pocket. I'd memorized the names and Googled the drugs from my phone. I watched him lie to me and tell me they were for sleep deprivation. It was only then that I realized we were never going to end up together. Months and months went by. I was holding on to nothing.

## Matterhorn

*After Andre Breton's "Free Union"*

My husband whose eyes are glowing auburn crystals

Whose eyes are like crying canopies

Canaries the color of sweet cocoa cranberries

Whose eyes are telling the sunset how

A giant telepathic ellipsis between just us

My husband whose eyes are undressing me every
moment

Whose lips are like kissing watercolors

Whose saliva is sorbet gelato waterfalls

Whose saliva is an elixir betwixt my treasure pillow

Whose tongue is a swimming dolphin set free

Whose fingers are slivering snails on a park slide

Whose arms are hedges that form labyrinths to get lost in

Whose arms are for catastrophic days that come to play quite often

Whose biceps are solid rock pears

My husband whose collarbone whispers I love you

I can hear it way in the kitchen

Whose chest has the richness of my birthday and Christmas

Whose chest is Teddy Ruxpin in denial

My husband whose breath is an avalanche of determination

Whose breath is my ricochet I plummet into a somersault

I perfectly land it.

Whose stance is a callous

Whose stance is a kite flying conversation in the middle of the night

Whose hands are body builders' boulders

Whose hands are kickstands, I meant quicksand, on my shoulders

Whose shoulders are campaigns to curb loneliness

Whose smell is laundry room powder running over

Whose smell is the melted remnants of a soap dish

The smell of a blushing sunrise and tuxedos in the morning,

Whose smile is my first choice premonition.

Whose smile is untitled.

Whose chin is a summer spring glacier.

My husband who is brave like white gold.

Whose soul is an envelope holding the letters to our stories,

Sweet like Jarritos, homemade like pupusas, warm like a bath and a roof.

Made of detours and maps, of candied candle wax.

Whose love is knocking over track stars in ski masks.

Whose love is suspended on windowsills and fireplaces.

Whose love is my undertaking three lives from now,

two worlds ago, and the ice that melts to water to keep me alive

My husband whose concentration is chess and restless arguing over background music

Whose voice is the mount, no matter who wins,

Whose lungs are the dragon's calm in and out breathe in and in

My husband whose penis tastes of pineapple peach
soymilk

sends me flying to Hong Kong every orgasm since

My legs are perfect origami early every morning

Whose lovemaking creates alternate worlds

Whose lovemaking stills my universe

but shakes this ground.

My husband with so many questions

I have so little patience

Whose dreams are whirling weightless

For him, I'd build a snow mountain taller than the Eiffel

He'd slide down the white Slurpee wearing nothing but a
towel

—superhero style

My husband whose heart is the size of the Matterhorn

You have been every dream I have been scared to say out loud.

*

You are the only one I could ever really see it with; I don't even think I want it now.

*

When I went to visit him at our old house to get the last of my items out of the garage, I saw he'd thrown the basket of keepsakes away. The keepsakes of our relationship: The Complete Mess Collection. Every picture, every poem, every journal, every ticket stub, and memory pamphlet—everything somebody who loved you would have saved. I'd purposely left it in our house thinking he'd see it and realize he shouldn't have let me go. He'd thrown everything away. He never wanted to be my husband, and that was what I was going to have to understand.

\*\*\*

I wish it had been enough. My new job. My new apartment without him. It only made me want the family I lost *more*. It only made me want someone who wouldn't hurt me *even more.*

"I think this breakup, this you moving out—this, you know, I think it'll make us better people," Mike said to me the month after I moved out.

I didn't respond, I just thought to myself angrily a lot: *Now this fuckjob wanted to celebrate being debt-free— soon enough, brag about moving in with his brother and paying less than $600. Now he wanted to go rattle off about buying a few condos and how much "richer" he was gonna be without having to pay the ridiculously high "rent" for a house we only moved to because of our kids. Make us better people, huh? What the fuck? For the world? Get the fuck outta here. We were supposed to be better people for each other. This was the same man who*

*used to whisper how much he wanted to spend the rest of*
*his life with me, that he'd do anything for me. The man*
*who said everything was "ours" but meant everything*
*was "his" because he'd paid for it. The man who said*
*he'd never loved anyone more and couldn't live without*
*me. He was living without me; he was fine; in fact, he*
*only cared about himself.*

The first weekend after I moved out, Mike was
working a job in downtown LA, and he offered for me to
come down and stay with him at a hotel so he could work
*and* spend time with me. My stomach fluttered. I ended
up on the rooftop of said hotel, negating my writing
responsibilities, and then later making some of the best

love we hadn't made in years. I say this without shame because we'd actually become friends, which transcended to roommates in a real sense.

A few days later, he sent me some song about thinking and dreaming of me.

I sent back a text:

**ME:** DO YOU EVEN THINK OF ME? DO YOU *REALLY* DREAM OF ME?

**MIKE:** I DO NOW... YOU KNOW, SINCE YOU LEFT. BUT WHEN YOU WERE HERE, *NAH*, I NEVER DID.

"The One" Actually Is:

Someone who loves not just you—but your mission. Someone who has fallen in love with your passions so much they've made them their own, as you have theirs. This is someone who understands if you don't date selfishly, you can't love selflessly. You have to have enough in common with that person, so it doesn't feel you are going too far beyond yourself to love them. Since physical attraction is a given, you must have enough differences from each other to feel challenged and intrigued emotionally and mentally.

That person must be willing to teach you;

you must be willing to learn.

*

The Friday I received the keys to my new apartment, I was fired from my new job on the technicality that what the company had hired me to do was different than anything they'd let on. It was the first time in my life I'd been let go, without warning, and I had no idea what I was going to do. Yes, I was crazy to have even gone through with it, but the new place had beautiful dark hardwood floors, full amenities, and a second room I could use as a closet. I was running into a wall with him, and I needed my own space.

I had little savings but was determined to show him I didn't *need* him, although the truth was, financially, I did. I could survive without him in a basic way, but to thrive without him wasn't going to happen without a major job or life shift. After so many years, I didn't want to be with anyone who didn't want me as much as I, *him*. It was degrading, and I knew it, but I had to keep trying. It was too hard to let go of the years.

To quote Mae West, sex is an emotion in motion. I just wasn't quite sure which emotions we had left. In order for me to find The One, I'd have to have let someone in, but when I arrived at our door, it still opened with my key... he hadn't changed the locks. I was so exhausted from life that I hadn't slept in weeks. I had no time or intention to find anything but sleep and the love I already knew I wanted.

I plopped myself down across our old couch and closed my eyes for a second. His hand slid up the back of my spine. Warm and large and perfect. Hours must have passed, I opened my eyes, and it was dark out of the window. He tapped me and whispered for me to get up and go lie in the bed.

"Oh, the mattress, you mean?" I giggled back.

"Less is too much," he said back.

He had only two blankets, but he wrapped me in both, arms full and wide around me like I'd wanted most for the last few years and in moments I was moaning—an hour later—sleeping like I'd been looking for a new morning and had found it.

We'd resorted to really great and incredibly emotional sex since I'd left, which made him really just an almost nine-year version of a mind-fuck. In the last year I'd thought we were together we might have had sex less than ten times; I beg to say it was even eight. He was not much different than he was when we met—no better. Nonetheless, *I* was different now, and now I knew everything he hadn't disclosed.

I wasn't just fearful of every relationship and the possibility of it being pulled from under me like a rug. I was fearful because—for me—there simply was no floor for me at all.

"OUT OF THE SAD SACK OF SAD SHIT

THAT WAS MY LIFE,

I MADE A WORDHOUSE."

- LIDIA YUKNAVITCH

The only thing I had left was words. It was the only thing I could find through the confusion. Anything that didn't hurt as much as the last was an upgrade to me.

Hearsay

To love: you'd better float.

Love—you'd better fly.

Godspeed into promises and good-byes.

He said: Tell me how hard it is...

I said: when you're lying in bed,

And silent tears swell up and fall—

When you didn't tell them to at all.

He said, baby, someone else's love can't make you

happy.

You have your own happy place.

I said: He made love to me.

And whatever it lacked, he enhanced at a slow pace.

And I swear it didn't make sense. I thought it was
actual happiness.

I wasn't just happy—I was weightlessness happening.

He said: you can't love anybody that big.

I said: I did.

Yeah, I'm sure of it. I did.

*

Months later, I realized I was still somehow logged into his email. I received an email that was clearly meant for him, in the name of a woman he'd claimed he was never with. It was a brand-new bill he'd gotten in her name. Eventually, curiosity got the best of me, and I found out what I'd already known to be true—the part I'd so long ignored—the relationship he had been in with another person. He'd talked about her a lot, but in the way of her being just a "friend," someone he'd make investments with… all that mattered now was someone who had lots of money, not me.

This new space of *not-love* was the worst space I'd ever been in... for several reasons. One, because it was over and had been over for quite some time, and it was only a combination of sheer denial (on my end) and trickery (on his end) that led me to believe anything different. And two, because there was a part of me that had to admit I still wanted what he'd promised me in the beginning: forever. And lastly, because I couldn't say there were no red flags—flags were bright red and everywhere—it was just that I didn't want to see them fluttering, and I loved beyond every single one of them.

My dad had inadvertently taught me to stop waiting. Stop settling. To stop wishing and go get it. He died before most of the wishes I had for him or me could come true. He'd taken me to Hawaii countless times as a child, but I couldn't remember. Just once, as an adult, I wanted us to go there together. All I could think of over and over was: Why didn't I take him there, and what the fuck had I been waiting for?

That week Dad passed Mike was cold and had little to say. I didn't even consider him much of a friend through it. My eyes filled with water, and I floated the room, and when he did speak to me, I was ghostly or lashing out. I couldn't understand why he couldn't excuse me from entertaining his family and friends at a time when I'd suffered the worst loss of my life. What I came to understand was that his lack of empathy existed because he'd spent years *not caring.* He'd spent years preparing for what he knew all along. I'd spent those same years convincing myself that we weren't The Complete Mess Collection we were.

I saw, felt, and analyzed the ways in which each person broke me. It would take a man stronger than a kingdom to hold the weight I held, and his knees would lock, even still, while he buckled. I was too heavy. I had to get good at holding myself up.

The only reason I kept on was that I'd mastered the art of *wishing for it even when I couldn't see it happening.* It was a way of balancing. It was the type of resiliency that kept me moving forward but wouldn't keep me fully alive. I was still wishing, and even though it was like treading water slowly, it was all I knew.

One day, nearly half a year later, I left my job early and dizzy on an overcast afternoon and fainted (or fell asleep) on the freeway.

I'd woken up seconds before a semitruck roared on his horn as I swerved over—but I swerved too hard and fast, and my car spun backward facing the opposite direction of traffic. A swirl of colors was all I saw, spinning and spinning and cars moving in slow motion, but so damn fast. Horns blared, tires etched and screeched. A few cars to the left and right of me stopped entirely, enveloping me in a safe bubble. If those people in those cars around me had all not been driving *for me*, I would have likely lost my life and killed many others. I shook up and pulled to the side lane.

After talking myself through my breathing exercise, it took me twenty minutes to beg the lanes to merge back into traffic.

Between my 2.5-hour commute (both ways) and impossible marketing solutions, the on-call nurse said I was exhausted. She watched as my arms shook and told me she wanted to "run a few more tests," but she believed I just… needed rest.

When the doctor entered, he asked a few basic questions, and I gave him a synopsis. He stared into the center of my eyes uncomfortably… gave me a concerned look and said short and flatly,

"Oh, I think you're just sad."

# CHAPTER 9

# DREAMCATCHER

I'd been trying to reach my dreams from my tippy-toes. Studying where I'd lost me. Self-care. Plowing through workbooks and audiobooks, recognizing and managing triggers. I was guarded but confident. I attended a lot of classes: interval training sessions, Pilates, art shows, more writing groups, reading groups, definitely poetry, healing, sharing, growing.

This was how it started, and this was how I met him. He was misplaced in my mind. He came along at a time when my heart was so broken inside of shock and disbelief that I believe I made him up on some days. Other days, he was real to me.

He had dark hair and tight eyes, full lips, full brows, fit. He was a daydream off the deep end. It was quite possible I'd gotten stuck in the wish. The wish didn't come with a night-light.

I wanted him to love me from the very second I saw him, but I couldn't balance that little inkling of fear that sat between hoping for it and giving up on believing in it at all, not to mention believing it could be him.

In the daydream, I'd fumble my words. I made awkward advances. I left abruptly every chance I got. Far from infatuation—I had a real, butterfly-dancing, throat-lumping, stutter-stuck stare-crush of no other sort. I'd been so sure I could never feel that way again.

He became the perfect muse—living only vicariously in my desires because I feared him not feeling the same. Actually, it was more like a daymare. As it happened, all I could feel was each person I'd loved and how they'd hurt me—*beyond hurt*. If he had been sure, I would have broken my rules.

One night, I had a lucid dream, and my world stalled. He was in the pictures I'd painted in poems, but this time, the pictures were moving.

We were in paradise. I asked if I could shower—there was sand in my toes. I should've known then. He said all was ok in minimal words. It was quiet, and the sunset overlooked the ocean through the wall-to-wall hotel window. His face beamed beautifully, but he was mostly as dark as I was inside, and from the second I arrived, I knew it. I sighed.

He'd been my muse for a while. Too intensely good to be true. We lay on our sides, facing each other forehead to forehead. In and out, out and in—breathing the same air.

He felt so soft.

I couldn't read through his calm like a loss of signal.

We kissed. Wetness seeped between my thighs.

He whispered for me to breathe slower.

I slowed. He melted into me, and I didn't bother thinking.

What would the thinking have been for?

For the first time in my life, I let myself feel—

*everything.*

"It's a little bit more than a crush," I said as he was moving inside of me.

…He slid out.

MY WISH AT THAT MOMENT WAS THAT

HE WOULD KNOW WHAT IT IS.

...

SO WHENEVER HE FELT IT AGAIN,

HE WOULD KNOW WHAT IT WAS.

We sat up quickly.

# DREAMCATCHER

I WOULD FOREVER CHASE THAT MOMENT—

NOT THE FOREVER.

*YOU CAN'T CATCH FOREVER.*

A dreamcatcher caught my wish and slid down its feathers just in that second. I gasped and held my breath as everything slipped. I was caught in the web of it now. Even my fantasies were moonlit tragedies.

\*

"Ssssh… don't talk," he said in the shower as he washed me up. Everywhere. My back—gently. Between my legs—slowly. I held on to the railing. He wanted nothing, but I wanted everything.

"If it were going to be something, it would have already been something." He spoke again—calmly. Ah, a shooting star just blew it.

I pinched myself on the outside of my hand, but I couldn't feel it. Right, *dreaming.* I pretended I knew better, but I hadn't. This had never happened to me before.

We hugged twice. I left walking in the dark and got lost on the way back.

I would've done it, again and again, hoping for a different path.

"IT IS OUR IMAGINATION THAT IS

RESPONSIBLE FOR LOVE,

NOT THE OTHER PERSON."

- MARCEL PROUST

## Sugar to Shit

You are inside me. And this.

This world is of no other world.

It's sucrose and spoils.

Sugar to shit.

\*

I want the way I feel about you to *keep feeling about*

*you*, present tense.

No dream state. Just as intensely. I don't want to feel

any way other than this.

It's breathing the way I need you.

Like, breathing.

\*

Like dreams waking up every morning from the

fucking sky.

You are inside me.

A figment of my own, magical quiet.

And I could swear I died, but I am very much alive.

*

You are sitting in my mind.

You're twiddling your fingertips around the front of

your lips.

And it's sugar now.

Your temperament is nonexistent.

*

Your smile is looking at me like a small child.

Clouds are forming in my chest.

Sun warms my collarbone.

Joy is toiling my lobe; it says, "You like a boy. *You*

*like a boy.*"

\*

But then… our temporary is over.

Our time is limited to just a while.

I leave, and I breathe heavier, and we don't speak,

and I keep a little piece of impossible until I see you

again, it's that dream still.

*

And I know you're my person, but it's turned to shit,

or worse…

It's invisible, or worse, it just hurts too much to know

you.

*

And I don't even know you.

You don't even exist.

Sugar to…

…

Have you made a wish yet?

I think it's time you made another wish.

# DREAMCATCHER

YOU WANNA SEE IT IN REAL LIFE?

DO NOT CLOSE YOUR EYES ON THE RIDE.

The thing about caring about a person is that there's always a chance you could have been wrong and you could lose at some point. That potential loss is a chance you'd have to be willing to take. It's always about how fast you can back get up. I was stuck in my imagination for months.

The faster you can get back up after you've been let down, the more time you have left to find someone more worthy, the more time you have left to make better use of your time, the more time you have left…

Some experiences are extraordinary because they show you what's possible. Not because they're meant for you.

# DREAMCATCHER

HE HAD DONE SOMETHING THAT NO ONE

HAD EVER DONE BEFORE.

HE INSPIRED ME TO DREAM AGAIN.

If he'd been real, I would have told him I felt so much, and even though I couldn't prove "*it*," however "*it*" was, and whatever "*it*" did, it somehow infiltrated my system and moved inside of my body so much I couldn't *not* feel it—in energy.

Proof I never needed it to exist in real life.

Proof I could have it.

Proof it was possible.

Proof it doesn't save you.

Proof it doesn't "change you" *unless you allow it to.*

And I felt him more after I let go of the idea than when I'd thought it could come true.

YOU WILL NOT DIE

FROM FEELING EMOTIONS;

THEY HURT MORE WHEN YOU DENY THEM

THEIR OWN ROOMS IN YOU.

"But you can't hold your breath. Breathing is the most

important part."

## Not Breathing

Breathe with me whenever you're ready I'm
whisperlillies I'm not never ready
you got me good in between the heart and the shoulda
couldas…

I can't. Cause all I think about is ever after ~ after,
everything.
That place we got stuck in loving me like a dance in a
trance some luck in a dream state.

So that was it, that's where you came from,
That's why I can't reach you.

You aren't real and it's ok, I'm overstanding.
It's just that if you ever wanna love you gotta gamble.
~I gave all my hands fill~

Out in lavender fields, picked till my hands bled... it's a standstill.

It's really a landfill.

I'm digging up weeds under windmills.

I'm begging please as the tears slip.

It's a fine line between finders keepers.

Lalie, you don't get to keep this one.

Losers, dreamers.

See~ers?

See it's a fine night for a finite trip across the sky right?

I wished on you well in allllll my daddy's wishing wells.

As soon as I reached out—you breached.

I ran back in cuz geesh I'm scared to get hurt again.

Guess we'll just be friends; or pretend?

That's how it all ends up anyway.

Overheard the faeries ask you:
You gon' let a wildfire get away?

He can't believe it's real
But some things you gotta feel…


I went dark. Agoraphobic. Weeks in the house with

little contact. I stopped everything. Nothing else had ever,

ever been a dream so exact.

It was true. You had to know dark to be light.

Career coaches would say that when opportunity,

education, and skill met my goals, I'd be successful.

Motivational entrepreneurs would say I had to work for it

harder than I wished for it. What everyone failed to say

was that I could prep, wish, and work and still *not get it.*
So what I had to grow was balance and resilience. I had
to allow myself to accept the bad without denying it, and
I had to praise the good without fearing happiness. I had
to balance the two and remember to bounce back without
any apology.

I wrote this book for everyone like me, afraid their
dreams were nightmares, for everyone scared of heights.
For everyone afraid to wish for it. Everyone who would
look into the skyline unable to understand why certain
things happened, why other things couldn't. For everyone
in the hurt of love. Scratching the surface and waiting,
trying to reach the part that allows you to trust.

COME THROUGH, BABY,

THE DREAM IS STUCK.

Next time, I don't want you to be some dream I

made up.

This shit sucks.

# DREAMCATCHER

"FOR TO WISH TO FORGET HOW MUCH YOU
LOVED SOMEONE--AND THEN, TO ACTUALLY
FORGET-CAN FEEL, AT TIMES, LIKE THE
SLAUGHTER OF A BEAUTIFUL BIRD WHO
CHOSE, BY NOTHING SHORT OF GRACE, TO
MAKE A HABITAT OF YOUR HEART. I HAVE
HEARD THAT THIS PAIN CAN BE CONVERTED,
AS IT WERE, BY ACCEPTING "THE
FUNDAMENTAL IMPERMANENCE OF ALL
THINGS." THIS ACCEPTANCE BEWILDERS ME:
SOMETIMES IT SEEMS AN ACT OF WILL; AT
OTHERS, OF SURRENDER. OFTEN I FEEL
MYSELF TO BE ROCKING BETWEEN THEM
(SEASICKNESS)."

- MAGGIE NELSON

If I had confessed, I loved someone I never really

knew, he would have just said, "How would you love

what you don't know?"

\*

To which I might have replied,

"No one *knows* anyone really, *ever.*"

\*

This I hold as truth.

We are all ever changing.

*

And we felt something *we both knew*—we both knew.

Something so real we didn't know what to do with it.

*

What really happened, you don't ask?

I saw him as nothing else than what it had to be when

he had no reaction.

A pivot point I'd just imagined.

But that's just if it happened.

I have no idea what to do with what never happened.

# DREAMCATCHER

"MY FATHER TOLD US STORIES ABOUT THE MAGIC FISH THAT WOULD GRANT US ANYTHING WE WISHED FOR. THE SECRET OF THE MAGIC FISH WAS THAT BY THE END OF THE STORY, EVERY SINGLE TIME, WE WOULD REALIZE WE HAD WISHED FOR THE WRONG THING. IF WE ASKED THE FISH FOR AN ENDLESS BAG OF CANDY, WE WOULD GET CANDY THAT WAS SO DISGUSTING WE WOULD BEG THE FISH TO TAKE IT BACK."

- EULA BISS

Daddy used to say, "Nobody is going to help you get over it, and nobody cares." There were some dreams I would have that would never be fully realized, and that was ok. Some dreams would always be up too high for me to reach. Some people would give you a boost up, and some would watch you stumble.

Be careful where you put your attention.

*That* is your power.

Once you have given a particular part of you, there simply was not an easy way to get it back.

You may not be the same person before your dream as you are after.

DREAM SLOWER.

You never needed permission.

# CHAPTER 10

# WISH PROOF

To trust someone with everything I'd been through was just too much to be able to explain and hope they understood. I wrote it all down and blew flyaway dandelions. I applied what I'd learned about wishes and heartbreak to myself:

Was being fearless just another one-day-at-a-time mantra? I wanted it, but all I thought of were the times I'd spent with my father, who'd done nothing in his last years of life but regret all he didn't do, all he didn't have, and *everything he'd wished for*.

We were the same.

But every lesson Dad taught me was in every mistake he made. Balance sleep, but remember not to sleep too much. Breathe. Balance the wish, but remember not to wish too much. Believe it. All I had to do was study how to heal myself, how to swing on the swings.

Catch the wind in your momentum.

Chase everything you don't get to keep.

All I had to do was make life more real to me than my dreams.

*

I read red flags like reflexes. What you go through doesn't get easier or make you stronger, I've found; it makes you familiar with pain. Being familiar with pain can go two ways. It can make you build up a resiliency or a fear—your choice. Sometimes both. Sometimes at different moments within the same day.

Life is, as said by many, a *Choose Your Own Adventure* book. The result could be a person who became stronger. That part isn't easy or immediate.

# WISH PROOF

ALWAYS WISH FOR IT.

EVEN WHEN YOU HAVE NO PROOF.

EVEN WHEN YOU'VE LOST YOUR BALLOON.

EVEN WHEN ALL YOU CAN DO IS FEEL

YOUR WAY THROUGH.

Becoming familiar with the stories I told myself when I was in pain gave me strength. I could anticipate myself: I was going to go dark and want no one around. I had to keep people around but be alone long enough to still feel everything enough to heal, recognize, and take steps to rebuild in an improved way.

Balance.

Always make a wish list because that's where the start is.

Even if you don't have any way to get there or any real proof anything you believe in–really exists.

Sometimes you can love so much that to save yourself, you have to leave, even if leaving will leave you with nothing.

Keep writing the wish list, even though everyone's gone.

# WISH PROOF

*ALWAYS WISH TOO HIGH UP.*

WHEN YOU FALL, YOU'RE GONNA LAND

WHERE YOU'LL BLOOM.

The morning my dad passed away, there was a
moment I felt him, like a quiet chill tickling through me. I
like to make up things I think he would have said to me, I
want to tell myself there were things I should have said,
but my father was my best friend. He knew everything
about me. There was nothing more I needed to say
because every day I told him I loved him, and every day
he told me he loved me. I knew only a fraction about him:
his life was so full. The stories he told me were filled
with detailed regret; I remember them vividly, like books.
He told me about a woman he loved once, but he could
never have her. He believed she loved him too, but he
said they did not see each other much.

As he got older, he told me this story over and over, each time the same with more detail. The flowers in her light blue dress were more vibrant; her hair blew in the wind as they zipped by in his drop-top convertible. She was so important to him, and yet he never advanced at her aside from the instance he'd replay to me over and over of her riding with him in his car. It's hard to call him a liar while each time I uncovered more pieces of his story, and it was like I could see the fair-skinned woman, as bright as she was through his eyes. He said she was elegant, and her perfume was like heaven. He described the way she was put off by him trying to fix her dress, as if she thought he was trying to look under it. They continued to flirt on and on. It never went anywhere.

Each time my dad told this story, this woman became more intriguing to me. I tried many times to ask her name—maybe I could find her? Reunite them? Perhaps she was married, or not. Even so, at his age, it couldn't hurt much for an old man to see an old friend?

After he passed, I would tell people I was doing fine, elaborating stories of being busy, fanciful nights I partied—when I really was in bed, reading, or slumped over the book as I fell asleep. Sometimes I would curl up into a ball, waiting for Dad's death to kill me. Just me and my tissues in my new apartment alone... Falling asleep breathing into Dad's old blanket and sniffing the last of his smell from his old faded green shirt. It could have been true, that this woman Dad so vividly dreamt of, who hadn't been my mother, who had no name, whose whereabouts were unknown—it could have been that she was just a dream. A wish he couldn't get to.

It was then I realized how much the longing for someone could create a reality that may not have ever been there. The experience could have been jaded entirely. The craving would get so strong that you could live off the fantasy itself. She could have been a woman, or our family that stayed together, or the house he should have bought or shouldn't have lost. She could have been any wish that had ever come and gone. But that hope kept him: *still*.

YOU GET TO KEEP THE STORY.

THE STORY. IT'S *YOURS*.

I thought about everyone I've ever loved. Of every wish I've ever wished for. Everything I'd ever wanted was in my stories. Like a quiet chill shooting through me, again. I woke up.

I'm up now. I'm up.

I fell back into the only comforter and pillow I'd bought since I moved, grabbed my notebook, and wrote the last wish I would ever wish on and not get.

# WISH PROOF

I KNOW IT'S ALL GONE

AND THAT FEELS SO HOPELESS.

BUT I STILL WISH YOU WERE HERE.

HOWEVER EVER AFTER...


THE END.

# ACKNOWLEDGMENTS:

Daddy. Daddy. Daddy. Daddy. Daddy. Daddy. Daddy. My reason.

Mama. Tye Julian. Ree Ree. Olivia Leraé. Victoria Michelle. Donovan Winston.

Mommy Cheryl. Terry. Dale. Marc. Michael David. Eric. Richea. Kristin. Sandra. Euna. Lloyd. Tisha. Devin. Sasha. Rese. Jasmine. Melissa. Trenishia. Nikki. Jason.

Matthew Daddona. Kelly Cozy.

Everyone who has supported me, you are proof some wishes do come true.  I love you.

And for everyone who gave up on me, *perfect timing.* Also Henry. Evan. Liam. Dylan. Mike. And My Muse. Thank you for everything you gave me to use. It's now in the world so it can heal someone.

[Blows a kiss in the air and sends soup and a get well soon card]

Bloom,

Lalanii

CPSIA information can be obtained
at www.ICGtesting.com
Printed in the USA
BVHW042231071219
565855BV00029B/709/P